COMMUNICATION:
Your Key to SUCCESS

UNLOCK THE SECRETS THAT WILL INCREASE
PRODUCTIVITY AND PROPEL YOU TO A BRIGHTER,
MORE FULFILLING FUTURE

ST Training Solutions
Success Skills Series

SHIRLEY TAYLOR
& ALISON LESTER

COMMUNICATION:
Your Key to SUCCESS

UNLOCK THE SECRETS THAT WILL INCREASE
PRODUCTIVITY AND PROPEL YOU TO A BRIGHTER,
MORE FULFILLING FUTURE

Marshall Cavendish
Business

© 2009 Marshall Cavendish International (Asia) Private Limited
© text Shirley Taylor and Alison Lester
© series title Shirley Taylor
Illustrations by Edwin Ng
Cover art by Opal Works Co. Limited

Published by Marshall Cavendish Business
An imprint of Marshall Cavendish International
1 New Industrial Road, Singapore 536196

Other Marshall Cavendish Offices
Marshall Cavendish Ltd. 5th Floor 32–38 Saffron Hill, London EC1N 8FH · Marshall Cavendish Corporation. 99 White Plains Road, Tarrytown NY 10591-9001, USA · Marshall Cavendish International (Thailand) Co Ltd. 253 Asoke, 12th Flr, Sukhumvit 21 Road, Klongtoey Nua, Wattana, Bangkok 10110, Thailand · Marshall Cavendish (Malaysia) Sdn Bhd, Times Subang, Lot 46, Subang Hi-Tech Industrial Park, Batu Tiga, 40000 Shah Alam, Selangor Darul Ehsan, Malaysia

Marshall Cavendish is a trademark of Times Publishing Limited

National Library Board Singapore Cataloguing in Publication Data

Taylor, Shirley.
    Communication : your key to success / Shirley Taylor & Alison Lester. – Singapore :
    Marshall Cavendish Business, c2009.
    p. cm. – (Success skills series)
    Includes index.
    ISBN-13 : 978-981-261-675-3 (pbk.)
    1. Business communication. 2. Interpersonal communication.
    I. Lester, Alison Jean. II. Title. III. Series: Success skills series (ST Training Solutions)

HF5718
651.7 — dc22   OCN373680800

Printed in Singapore by Times Printers Pte Ltd

ACKNOWLEDGEMENTS

Communication is our lifeblood, and it's the lifeblood of every organisation, so I consider this book to be the very heart of the Success Skills series. As such, I'd like to take this opportunity to thank several people who have been influential in bringing this exciting series to life.

First of all, many thanks to Violet Phoon and Chris Newson for your confidence, support and enthusiasm right from the start. Thanks also to Mei Lin, Mindy and Stephanie for your expertise in the editorial process and for your endless patience. Thanks also to the designers, Bernard Go and Benson Tan, plus the whole team at Marshall Cavendish in Singapore. I'm very grateful for all your help, and thank you in advance for your support as the Success Skills series grows.

My thanks too to the team at Pansing Distribution, in particular my dear friends Leslie Lim and David Buckland, who have been very influential in my publishing career for many years.

Kudos to Edwin Ng, the talented man behind the superb illustrations in all the books in the Success Skills series. What a fantastic talent you have, Edwin, and the pages of these books are much richer for your contribution.

I'm very grateful to all the authors of current and future books in the Success Skills series. Through ST Training Solutions, I'm very fortunate to work with some very talented trainers, and I'm learning from them all the time. I'm so pleased that I now have the opportunity to extend our collaboration by building up this Success Skills series.

Personal thanks to Alison Lester and Heather Hansen, authors of two of the first books in this series, for your friendship, support and encouragement. You are two real stars!

Shirley Taylor.

PREFACE

Congratulations on picking up this copy of *Communication: Your Key to Success*. I'm very proud that this is one of the first books in the ST Training Solutions Success Skills series. This series includes several short, practical books on a range of topics that will help you develop your skills and enhance your success at work and in your personal life too.

The Success Skills series was originally created to meet the needs of participants of ST Training Solutions public workshops. After attending our workshops, many participants expressed a real desire to continue learning, to find out more about the topic, to take it to another level. They were hungry for knowledge. Just the effect I hoped for when I set up ST Training Solutions in 2007. With the Success Skills series of books, the experience and expertise of our trainers can be enjoyed by many more people.

As Series Editor, I've enjoyed working with the authors to make sure the books are easy-to-read, highly practical, and written in straightforward, simple language. Every book is packed with essential tools and strategies that will make you more effective and successful. We've included illustrations throughout that reinforce some key points, because I believe we learn more if we add some fun and humour. You'll also notice some key features that highlight important learning points:

Myth Buster   Here you will find a statement that is not true, with notes on the true facts of the matter.

Fast Fact   Useful snippets of information or special points to remember.

Aha! Moment

This is a 'light bulb' moment, when we note something you may be able to conclude from a discussion. Don't forget to note your own 'Aha! Moments' perhaps when you receive some extra insight that clarifies an important point.

Try This

Here you'll find a suggestion for how you can put a special point into practice, either at home or at work.

Danger Zone

You'll find some words of warning here, such as things to avoid or precautions to take.

Star Tips

At the end of each chapter you'll find a list of Star Tips — important notes to remind you about the key points.

By picking up this book you have already shown a desire to learn more. The solid advice and practical guidelines provided in this book will show you how you can really go from good to great!

Good luck!

Shirley Taylor

Shirley Taylor
Series Editor
CEO, ST Training Solutions Pte Ltd

 ST Training Solutions

www.shirleytaylortraining.com
www.shirleytaylor.com

Shape the Star in You!

Visit www.STSuccessSkills.com now to download your free e-book **'Your 7 Steps to Success'** containing motivating advice from our Success Skills authors. You can also read lots of author articles and order the latest titles in the Success Skills series.

CONTENTS

INTRODUCTION

Most people would agree that their satisfaction at work is largely derived from the way they, their colleagues and their clients communicate. The fundamental building blocks of successful communication involve being able to deliver a message clearly and engagingly, and to understand and appreciate other people's messages. This in turn leads to increased productivity and a sense of professional well-being.

Human communication tends to be a complicated affair, however. It's layered with unclear expectations, undisclosed hopes, and unfortunate misunderstandings.

Many young people actually start their working lives not knowing how to communicate face to face with their colleagues, let alone with employers and clients. They are more comfortable sending text messages than they are speaking. Some people lack the confidence to speak up when communicating, while others are so overconfident that they don't know how to listen. Then they wonder why they aren't given more responsibilities and are overlooked for promotion.

Luckily, successful communication skills can be learned, and help is right here in your hands! *Communication: Your Key to Success* provides practical, effective tools to help you increase clarity and understanding, improve confidence, enhance teamwork, boost productivity, and create a happier, more supportive working environment.

Excellent communication skills are probably the most potent career and personal skills you can possess. They can spell the difference between success and failure in getting your job done, and in building successful relationships personally and professionally.

In the pages of this book, we give solid guidance on the many aspects of successful communication, including listening skills, assertiveness, positive thinking, and much more. We offer straightforward advice and helpful examples, and we've even included some stories from our own lives — experiences that have helped us learn more about the intricacies and challenges of communication. We hope you enjoy these and, as we have done, learn from them.

Communication is our lifeblood, and it's the lifeblood of any organisation. As with any other endeavour, the more you put into it, the more you'll get back. This book is your starting point. Our goal has been to provide you with a fresh look at how you can transform your communication skills, and reap the huge rewards these changes will bring.

We hope you find the tools and guidelines useful. We are convinced that when you start putting them into practice, they will propel you along the path to a brighter, more fulfilling future.

Enjoy the journey!

Shirley Taylor
www.shirleytaylortraining.com
www.shirleytaylor.com
www.shirleytaylortraining.com/ASSAP
www.STSuccessSkills.com

Alison Lester
www.ajlestercommunication.com

ASSESS YOURSELF

What is your current approach to communication?

1. I know I'm making myself clear when I speak because:

a) No one says anything.

b) People do what I tell them to.

c) I can see the responses on people's faces.

2. Assertive communication means:

a) Getting my way.

b) Making sure that I respect the rights of others as much as my own.

c) Shouting louder than the rest.

3. Cultural differences can be managed by:

a) Insisting that everyone behaves the same way.

b) Letting everyone behave in their own way.

c) Everyone making an effort to come to a common understanding.

d) Watching movies together.

4. It is important to be consistent in professional communication because:

a) Consistency leads to respect and trust.

b) Consistency is very dull, and therefore unthreatening.

c) No one likes change.

5. Sophisticated telecommunications have made communication much easier.

a) True

b) False

c) True and false

6. I need to put extra energy into my voice when speaking on the telephone because:

a) People have trouble hearing me.

b) It helps me remember what I need to say.

c) Some of our energy is lost when it travels across the phone connection, so I sound less enthusiastic than I actually am.

7. I should wait as long as possible before dealing with friction in the office because:

a) It might go away.

b) I don't want to offend anyone.

c) It's best to let other people deal with it.

d) That's what everyone else does.

8. Listening means staying absolutely quiet when others are speaking.

a) True

b) False

9. Teams benefit from agreed communication guidelines because:

a)   People are generally stupid.

b)   Guidelines make sure that the team members' expectations are in line.

c)   Guidelines reduce friction.

d)   All of the above.

e)   b and c.

10. When I feel very strongly about an issue concerning a colleague, it's best to:

a)   Speak to the other person immediately. That's what assertiveness means.

b)   Talk to all my colleagues about it.

c)   Send an e-mail and let them know straight away.

d)   Cool off first, think about it, and then deal with it appropriately.

Check out these answers to see how you fared.

1.   Silence when you speak is no guarantee of comprehension. The correct answer here is (c). If you're not getting a visual response, it's best to ask whether or not your listeners understand. You'll find a lot on how to structure your messages in Chapter 4.

2.   Assertive behaviour is not aggressive behaviour. If you understand that being assertive is about self-respect and respect for others, you will have answered (b). Look at Chapter 6 for more on the assertive approach to communication.

3. The most helpful answer here is (c). We can't expect our culture to take precedence over others, nor can we agree completely to adapt to the culture of others, as you'll see in Chapter 9.

4. We hope you answered (a). In professional communication, consistency isn't dull. It's very motivating! You can read about why it's so important in Chapter 2.

5. The answer here is actually (c), because while technological advances have brought us into immediate communication with most of the world, this also means we are required to communicate with many more types of people than in the past. Chapter 1 will spell this out for you.

6. It's true that telephone connections dampen our energy a bit. Also, we usually speak on the phone while sitting down, and are less dynamic as a result. So the answer to this question is again (c). Read Chapter 7 for more on telephone communication skills.

7. Did this question puzzle you? We hope so, because none of the answers is correct! In fact, as you'll see in Chapter 10, it's best to investigate and try to resolve friction as soon as you become aware of it.

8. Listening involves being silent, but that's only part of the story, so the answer is (b). Listening skills are so important that we've devoted an entire chapter to the subject. Check out Chapter 3.

9. Did you answer (e) to this one? Friction in teams can be reduced if there are common expectations and goals. Learn more about encouraging smooth team communication in Chapter 8.

10. We hope you answered (d). You will always thank yourself later for cooling down first before speaking or writing. Learn more about dealing with emotions, and using appropriate tone and body language, in Chapter 5.

WHY IS COMMUNICATION IMPORTANT?

1

"It's phenomenal what openness and communication can produce. The possibilities of truly significant gain, of significant improvement, are so real that it's worth the risk such openness entails."

Stephen R. Covey

Don't take communication skills for granted

We've all been communicating since the day we were born. Does this mean we don't have anything to learn about communication skills? Certainly not! Communication can be studied and continuously improved. Being able to communicate effectively is a great gift, yet I'm sure many people would agree that we often take it for granted.

Advances in technology over the last couple of decades have transformed the way we work, enabling us to communicate faster, more efficiently and more effectively. It's ironic, then, that this technological evolution has brought about a decline in the art of effective communication. E-mail has quickly become an essential means of communication with clients and colleagues. However, many of us would have to admit that we sometimes send an e-mail when we absolutely know it would be better to pick up the phone, or perhaps just walk over to a colleague's desk to pass on a message. (You too, right?) So it's no real wonder that with so many of us 'hiding' behind e-mail, we are damaging our own ability to communicate orally, be it on the phone or face to face. Overuse of e-mail is decreasing our effectiveness when we actually do open our mouths. Personal interaction is at the heart of developing truly effective business relationships. And developing relationships is what will make us more successful in business.

The power of speech and sight cannot be underestimated, but many young people are actually starting their working lives not knowing how to communicate with their colleagues, employers and clients. They are more comfortable sending text messages than they are speaking. Many people lack the confidence to speak up when face to face, let alone in groups or meetings. They don't know the right words to use or how to express themselves clearly. Then they wonder why they are not given more responsibilities and are overlooked for promotion.

Fast Fact

Employers understand the positive relationship between communication and an organisation's success. The ability to communicate effectively is therefore often listed as a required attribute in many job advertisements.

Every day, all day, we are communicating

Sometimes we forget that even when we choose to say nothing, we are still communicating something. Sitting at our desks, concentrating, we are saying, "I am focused on work." Staying quiet in a meeting, we are communicating anything from "I'm too shy" to "I need time to think" to "You're all a bunch of numbskulls." When we do choose to use words, either by speaking or by writing, we deliver a wide range of messages as well, some of which may be unintended.

These days, we are expected to speak up more than ever, liaising with colleagues and clients, peers and superiors, both by telephone and in person. With open-plan offices and so much emphasis on teamwork today, there is a lot to learn about communicating with other people. So with communication taking up almost 100 per cent of our working day, this should show us the vital importance of learning how to get it right. Whatever your job, your age or experience, developing your communication skills must be the top priority.

Aha! Moment

Even when I'm not aware of communicating, I am communicating. My silence speaks, my body speaks, my face speaks. Even my clothes speak. It will help me to be aware of what I'm saying when I'm not saying anything.

Why do *you* need effective communication skills?

There is a huge and very obvious difference between people who make an ongoing effort to improve their communication and those who feel they know what they need to know and will stick to it. What attitude does this second group of people take when things go wrong? Do they often blame other people? "If only *they* had expressed themselves more clearly. If only *they* had listened more carefully. If only *they* had said that in the first place. If only *they'd* asked questions when they weren't so sure." Sound familiar? Do you work with people like this?

Or, perhaps, are you yourself one of them? Probably not, since you're reading this book! But we wouldn't be human if we didn't sometimes try to blame other people for our own lapses. What makes the difference is becoming aware of when we do it, and learning to take responsibility for our own communication ups and downs.

So you need to improve your skills, quite simply, because absolutely everyone does. Communication is the heart of every organisation. Everything you do in the workplace results from communication. Therefore, good reading, writing, speaking and listening skills are essential if you are to complete tasks and achieve goals. As you develop your career, you will find various reasons why successful communication skills are important to you, for example:

- **To secure an interview.** You will need good communication skills to make sure your application letter is read and acted upon.

- **To get the job.** You will need to communicate well during your interview if you are to sell yourself and land the job you want.

- **To do your job well.** You will need to request information, discuss problems, give instructions, work in teams, interact with colleagues and clients. If you are to achieve co-operation and effective teamwork, good human relations skills are essential. Also, as the workplace is becoming more global, there are many factors to consider if you are to communicate well in a diverse environment.

- **To advance in your career.** Employers want staff who can think for themselves, use initiative and solve problems — staff who are interested in the long-term success of the company. If you are to be seen as a valued member of the organisation, it is important not just to be able to do your job well, but also to communicate your thoughts on how the processes and products or services can be improved.

 Try This

> Make an exhaustive list of the tasks and responsibilities of your job, and show yourself how many types of communication you are required to use each day. Each of these can be improved!

Communicating in an ever-changing workplace

When we, the authors, first started working, snail mail was the only mail! Then there was the fascinating introduction of telex, and then fax, which sped things up greatly. Along came e-mail, and suddenly we were sending messages in as close to real time as we thought possible — until the onslaught of instant messaging! It seems that this should be the apex of telecommunication development, but today's workplace is still in a constant state of change.

If we are to meet the numerous challenges we will inevitably face, effective communication is vital. Here are some of the key reasons why we need effective communication skills in this rapidly-changing workplace:

- **Advancing technology.**   The Internet, e-mail, fax messages, voice mail, instant messaging, teleconferencing, videoconferencing, wireless devices. All this technology has transformed the way we communicate: people can work together almost effortlessly whether they are in New York or New Zealand, Singapore or Seattle, Beijing or Bangkok; in a car, an office, a hotel or at home; even in an airport or an aeroplane. With every phone call or e-mail, your communication skills are revealed for everyone to see.

- **Global communication.** More and more businesses are now multinational, working on a global scale across national and international boundaries. Today's workforce includes increasing numbers of people from different ethnic backgrounds, either within the same office or working together between regions. If you are to communicate effectively in this environment, you must understand other people's backgrounds, beliefs and characters.

- **The information age.** With a vast increase in the amount of information in the business world, you must be able to make quick, effective decisions based on the information you receive. You must also know how to find, assess, process and communicate information efficiently and effectively. With so much information available, it is a constant challenge to get your recipient's attention so that they will read your message and respond appropriately.

- **Team-based business environments.** The traditional management hierarchy has changed, and team working is now the norm. In such team-based environments, it is important to study individuals and understand how groups work together. We must learn to listen and watch other people carefully so that we can interpret all the verbal as well as non-verbal cues we receive.

 Danger Zone

Just because you are on top of things now doesn't mean that things won't change. You have to be constantly examining every interaction and every communication, and seeking ways to improve. Learning more about effective communication will help you adapt quickly to changing environments.

To learn more about how to improve your interpersonal skills in this electronic age, read Heather Hansen's *Powerful People Skills*, also in the Success Skills series.

Let's consider the ways some very successful communicators go about the business of communicating.

What makes a great communicator great?

When we ask people to tell us who comes to mind when they think of a great communicator, we often get answers like Oprah Winfrey for her ability to identify with people and make them feel comfortable talking about their lives; Lee Kuan Yew for his success in motivating Singapore into its pre-eminent economic position in Asia; Mahatma Gandhi for the clarity and consistency of his commitment to the rights of his people; Steve Jobs for his ability to lead innovation and get his message across; not forgetting, of course, Shirley Taylor and Alison Lester!

What about you? Think for a moment about all the people you consider to be great communicators. They may be celebrities, politicians, speakers, people on television or in movies, or people in your personal or working life. Maybe you feel really connected when talking to your grandmother, or really understood and motivated listening to your tennis coach during practice.

 Try This

Think of people you consider to be effective communicators. What is it that makes them so effective? Note down all their qualities.

Take a moment to compare your list with ours. We're sure they're pretty similar.

A good communicator knows:

- his/her subject matter
- his/her strengths and weaknesses
- the appropriate words to use
- the most effective questions to ask

A good communicator has:

- a clear voice
- solid self-esteem
- energy, passion and enthusiasm
- good body language
- good listening skills
- clear summarising skills

A good communicator knows how to:

- use words that the listener can relate to
- keep an open mind
- adapt his/her approach when necessary
- make the listener feel comfortable and valued
- empathise with the listener
- give a considered response
- make connections and build rapport

It's a long list of skills, but don't worry! We'll be talking about all these things as we progress through this book, and will show you how you can improve your own skills in each of these areas.

If you are communicating with someone who possesses all the qualities you just noted down, imagine how you'll feel on the receiving end. Fantastic, right? You will understand exactly what the communicator meant. You will know exactly what you need to do. Everything will seem much clearer. You will feel confident to get on with your job. You will feel appreciated. You will feel motivated.

Myth Buster

I have lots of qualifications and am now studying for a Masters. This will serve me well for getting and keeping a job.

Think again! You can acquire great knowledge, but unless you can communicate it to others, it is of very limited value.

Benefits of effective communication

Just in case you need a bit more fuel to feed your fire, here are some of the many benefits that you and your organisation can achieve from effective communication:

Reduced:	Increased:	Better, smoother:
stress	productivity	decision-making
conflict	sales	problem-solving
rumours	profits	workflow
mistakes	motivation	relationships
misunderstanding	co-operation	professional image

Your working environment will be much better if everyone in the organisation works on their communication skills, but you'll also feel the benefits even if you are the only one actively working on them. Above all, you'll have the personal satisfaction of knowing that you are being responsible and positive, and taking your success into your own hands. Secondly, you'll find that many of your relationships will improve, and you'll be able to reassess those that don't. Finally, you may find that you are leading by example, and others will follow suit.

The five stages in the communication cycle

There are five main stages in the communication cycle. Naturally, things can go wrong at each stage, so it pays to take a look at this process in detail to avoid as much misunderstanding as possible.

Stage	Problems that can occur
1. The sender You are the originator of the message. The way you communicate your message can be affected by your: • attitude towards the person you will be communicating with and the situation • immediate surroundings • culture • emotions • job status • education • language skills	• You don't think before you speak or write. • You don't have a clear idea of what you want to say. • You don't understand the issue.
2. The message This is the idea you wish to communicate. It will comprise oral and/or written messages. In compiling your message, you must consider various factors: • what must it include? • how will it be interpreted? • how will it affect your relationship?	• You choose language that the reader will not understand. • Your tone is inappropriate. • Your point is unclear. • Your message is not well structured.

Stage	Problems that can occur
3. The medium The medium is the method you choose for your message, be it a face-to-face conversation, a phone call, an e-mail message, a text message, or a letter in the post. A key factor in choosing the appropriate medium may be the urgency of the message.	• You choose the wrong method. • Transmission is interrupted or distorted. • You send the message at the wrong time or to the wrong place.
4. The recipient The recipient will be affected by the same factors as the sender — attitudes, surroundings, culture, emotions, etc. The message may be distorted if the sender has not taken care to craft the message appropriately, resulting in it being misinterpreted. Culture and time differences also affect the risk of misinterpretation.	• The recipient's vocabulary or frame of reference doesn't correspond to the one you used in your message. • The recipient focuses on how you say something rather than on the message itself. • If the message is too long, the recipient may be too busy to focus on it, and may miss your point.
5. Feedback Without feedback, you will not know if the communication process has been successful. There could be an immediate response in oral communication, such as a nod or a smile in meetings.	• No feedback is received. • Feedback is received too late. • Adequate time is not allowed for feedback. • Feedback is distorted by emotion or circumstances.

Fast Fact

How well you communicate is determined not only by how well you say things, but by how well the things you say are received. Learning how others communicate will help you improve this.

The dangers of not communicating well

Some people work in such difficult environments that they feel making an effort to change will just be too exhausting. They're too busy. They're too stressed. Or they're too scared, and what they fear is the unknown. But when communication breaks down, all sorts of things can go wrong, and what's worse, these things can take a long time to fix, since they often have to be completely unpicked to be understood.

If you are still wondering if working on your communication is truly worth the effort, let's take a look at how much more risky it is to do nothing. By not improving, you open yourself up to a long list of potential problems:

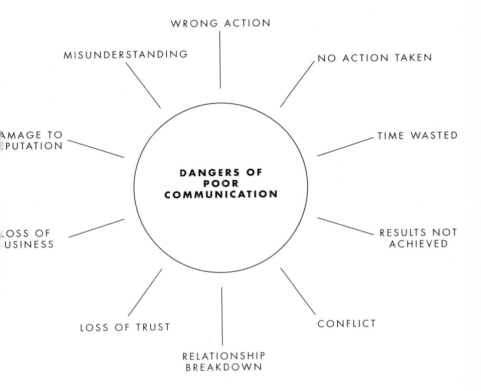

When communication breaks down for you, it has an effect on your team as a whole. A link in the chain is broken. Even an unresolved conflict between you and only one other colleague can have far-reaching effects in the business. People are sensitive, and the office will feel the tension. Doing what you can to maintain communication flow and effectiveness will benefit everyone. It's absolutely true that "A stitch in time saves nine"!

Aha! Moment

A breakdown in communication can lead not only to personal problems but also to problems for my organisation.

Myth Buster

Some people are just born great communicators.

It's unusual for someone to be endowed with all the attributes of a great communicator. You might naturally be a good listener, but weak in expressing yourself, while a good friend might be super at telling stories but quick to judge. Becoming a successful all-round communicator is always a work in progress.

Star Tips for understanding effective communication

1. Make a point to learn and continually develop your communication skills.

2. Develop better relationships by increasing your personal interaction.

3. Don't underestimate the power of speech and sight.

4. Avoid misunderstandings by considering each stage in the communication cycle.

5. Take care not to blame other people for your own communication weaknesses.

6. Remember that a breakdown in communication between two people can affect the whole organisation.

7. Don't let a first impression close your mind to the potential of a relationship.

8. Remember: you can speak volumes even when you don't open your mouth.

9. Adapt to your constantly changing work environment by aiming for effective communication skills.

10. Remember that improving communication is always a work in progress, and you will benefit from continual upgrading.

COMMUNICATION STARTS WITH YOU

2

"You can make more friends in two months by becoming interested in other people than you can in two years by trying to get the other person interested in you."

Dale Carnegie

Being likeable helps

If you are going to be an effective communicator and develop strong relationships, it's naturally an advantage if people like you and want to be around you. One of your aims must be to create an atmosphere of trust and openness. If you prefer to keep your head down in your job and maintain minimal relationships, that's fair enough. We're not asking you to change your personality. But if this is your way, you must recognise that it will be difficult for you to garner support from colleagues if you suddenly have an idea you want to push through.

Alison has a story to share about how communication affects professional relationships and effectiveness.

> I was hired to consult with an advertising company on their management team's communication skills. I quickly discovered that they were very antagonistic. Everyone was so intent on getting credit with their clients that they overlooked the company's internal health. They saw each other as obstacles rather than as human beings, and did little or nothing to smooth their interactions. They had no idea that the mother of one manager had just died, or that another manager's wife was expecting a child. Everyone felt lonely and unappreciated. I suggested that they hold a weekly meeting, first thing on Monday mornings, where they didn't have to set aside a big chunk of time but merely stood together in a huddle and told each other what was going on in their lives, both inside and outside the office. This would very likely lead to their following up with each other on these things later in the week, and feeling more like a team than like competitors as a result.

Even a little bit of effort to connect with the people around you can go a very long way. Shirley has a sweet story about the power of showing interest in others.

I often visit a stationery shop near my home. The older lady who works there is normally very welcoming and eager to help, but when I went in one day I noticed that she wasn't her usual self. She was sitting on a stool looking bored, tired, and fed up. We've chatted a little about our lives on other visits, so I asked her, "How's your lovely granddaughter?" Her face lit up and she cracked a big smile. She stood up, her body language changed, and she chattered away with stories about little Lena. Those few minutes brightened up her day, and of course the exchange made me feel good too.

Aha! Moment

Just like good manners, friendliness costs nothing, and is its own reward.

Let's start at the very beginning

If we are to learn how to communicate better, we must understand all the influencing factors that exist when we meet and interact with other people. We must also understand how these factors affect our communication and its outcome.

Fast Fact

When we meet someone new, we make a decision to classify that person within the space of a few seconds.

When we meet someone new, we form a nearly immediate opinion about them based on what our senses take in. All animals do this; it's part of our survival strategy. We're simply wondering if the person we are talking to is a friend or a foe. We have to watch out for being too rigid about these impressions, though, because we can take an instant dislike to someone who may actually benefit us, all because of the power of the external impressions we receive. If we don't keep an open mind and test the impression on another occasion, we can do them, and ourselves, a disservice.

Imagine you are meeting someone new for the first time. What do you think influences you when you make a decision about them? Take a moment to consider this.

Everything you see, hear, and even smell will have an effect on you. This includes:

- Appearance, including clothes, accessories and hygiene

- Physical characteristics, including height, weight, gender, race and age

- Body language, including posture, facial expressions, gestures, eye contact, and handshake or bow

- Voice, including tone, accent, pitch and pace

- Words

- Behaviour, including manners and attitude

- Personality

- Status

All of the things you see and hear when meeting new people will be put through your personal filter, which will include:

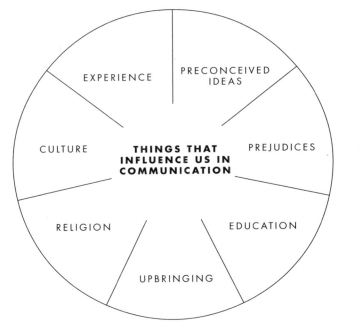

On top of all this, you will also be influenced by the situation and location of your meeting, and by your mood at that moment. It's a long list of influencing factors, but we are largely unaware of them as we go about our lives. For communication to be realistic and positive, we must make sure that the filters we have for classifying the people we meet and interact with aren't so finely woven that they limit the connections we are willing to make.

Danger Zone

Don't assume that your first impression is always the right impression.

It's important to develop a greater awareness of other people, learn to observe others carefully, and be more sensitive towards other people's emotions and attitudes.

Let's look at the important elements for ensuring that the people you want and need to communicate with get the right impression of *you*.

Authenticity

If you come across someone you feel is putting on an act, then you know what authenticity means: the opposite of what they are doing! Being authentic means being genuine, true to yourself, real. Being authentic means showing who you truly are, and to do this you must know yourself, your values and your purpose.

Myth Buster

It is important that our professional persona be different to our personal one.

Not so! People are generally more effective when they are authentic. Take regular reality checks to ask yourself "Who am I?", "What do I really feel and want?", "What do I really stand for?"

When you are authentic, your principles and personal values are clear, and you are willing to act on what truly matters to you. Authenticity means being able, truthfully, to use phrases like:

"I feel it is important that..."

"Here's what I think about this issue..."

"I don't agree with that because..."

"What really matters to me is..."

Once you are able to articulate these things to yourself, you can express them to others, and you can build working relationships that suit you and your goals.

How do you know if you are *not* being authentic? Here are some warning signs:

- You have lots of acquaintances and business cards, but very few real quality friendships or relationships.

- Your friendships are based on convenience and personal gain rather than on mutual benefit.

- Your actions depend on what is easy to go along with, rather than on what you really feel and what is right.

- You hide your true thoughts and feelings.

- You are not well respected in your community.

- When you compliment people, you come across as fake and false because you are saying something you don't really mean.

- You feel disconnected from what really matters to you.

 Try This

Write a list of what truly matters to you, your values. Type it out and stick it on your wall. For one month, keep track of any situations where you do or say things that contradict these values.

Danger Zone

"Be yourself" doesn't suggest "Go ahead and be mean if you feel like it."

Being authentic in a business environment involves managing yourself in a way that corresponds with your primary goals and principles.

The 3 C's of developing likeability

Your professional effectiveness will partly depend on how much people are willing to interact with you at work. You can't get your work done if people avoid you, can you? Consider these three C's, and whether or not they apply to you. Also, if there are people at work with whom you don't enjoy communicating, check if it's because they lack one of these characteristics, or more.

Credibility

Your credibility is the extent to which others believe what you tell them. Your success at work will very often depend on convincing people of your point of view. You need credibility for this, and the route to credibility is not only paved with knowledge and experience but also with *relationships*. If you are to make successful connections — connections that you can count on when you have new ideas and goals — you need to gain respect, create trust, and build rapport.

This won't happen if you consistently let others do the communicating in the office while you observe and judge. It won't happen if you engage in gossip and sneaky office politics. It won't happen if you are inconsistent in your responsibilities. It will also not happen if you are so rigid in your attitudes that you show unwillingness to listen and adapt. Credibility comes with transparency, engagement, and honest hard work.

 Try This

How credible are you? Ask yourself:

- Do I make an effort to keep my knowledge up to date?
- Do I turn up for meetings and share my knowledge?
- Do I get to know the people I work with?
- Do I keep others informed?
- Am I honest?

Consistency

Consistency and credibility go hand in hand. People tend to trust others who act in a consistent manner, and will avoid joining forces with those who don't follow their intentions with actions. If a staff member offers an idea in a meeting and you are welcoming, then the next day they speak up and you respond harshly, you'll be seen as unpredictable and your staff won't know if participating in meetings is safe or not.

An element of consistency is fairness. People who treat some colleagues in a very different way from others — for example being open to the ideas of favoured staff in meetings but not to everyone's ideas — are difficult to respect.

Only consistent people can expect consistent results from the people they communicate with. If you tend to act on whims, and insist your colleagues follow suit, don't be surprised if what they produce is as inconsistent as your own thinking.

Try This

Make a heading, 'Things I do consistently'. Then write down your list, including both positive and possibly negative items. For example, you could list that you are always on time for meetings. You could also list that you regularly buy coffee for one of the team's secretaries, but not for the other. Tick all the positive ones. Put a cross beside any negative ones. Ask yourself which of these things build trust? Which ones damage trust? Which ones are you willing and able to work on?

Confidence

When we ask participants at our workshops for a list of qualities of a great communicator, confidence is one of the first answers we get. Confident people know that they have something to offer in communication, and, just as importantly, they are open to what others have to offer as well. Employers want people with enough confidence to take full ownership of their job responsibilities as well as to take the risks involved in suggesting and implementing improvements.

Some people are concerned that self-confidence will come across as arrogance and therefore damage relationships. It's interesting to note that in fact, arrogance is often fear wearing a mask. Arrogant people, in their unwillingness to admit that others also have good ideas and achieve success, betray their concern for their own position. True confidence acknowledges other people's talents and skills, which is why confident people often make wonderful team players, and arrogant people do not.

Take a moment to see how you rate in this confidence quiz.

Score yourself the following points for each question:

Always = 5 points
Often = 4 points
Sometimes = 3 points
Rarely = 2 points
Never = 1 point

Your score	
	I like to take risks.
	I accept challenges willingly.
	I don't let fear stop me from doing things.
	I find it exciting to learn new things.
	I have a set of realistic goals.
	I don't berate myself when I make mistakes.
	I set my own values and don't allow others to influence me.
	I am willing to accept the consequences of my own behaviour.
	I follow my intuition when making decisions.
	I manage my money so that I have some left for enjoyment and savings.
	I like to keep everything organised.
	I balance my time between work and family, and keep some time free for me.
	I have good posture.
	I take time to exercise and eat properly.
	I have a wardrobe of clothes that I feel great wearing.
	I spend some time each day in quiet reflection.
	I have a spiritual outlet.
	I usually feel happy and positive.

	I have interests of my own and take time to pursue them.
	I have a group of friends that I enjoy being with.
	I enjoy meeting new people.

	YOUR TOTAL SCORE

98–105	Super-human self-confidence! Many congratulations! Share what you have with others!
77–97	High self-confidence. You are on the right track!
59–76	Average self-confidence. With some courage, you will surely develop.
43–58	Below-average self-confidence. You need a boost. Spend some time on improvement.
21–42	Low self-confidence. You will need to work hard on improving your self-confidence. It will take time, but you will see results.

This quiz is adapted from The Confidence Quiz, copyright Harriet Meyerson, founder of The Confidence Center in Dallas, Texas, USA. www.ConfidenceCenter.com.

Boosting your confidence

If you are someone with low self-confidence, how can you convince yourself that you are allowed to develop yourself in this area? The first, most powerful step is to start being aware of the thoughts in your head, and listening for negative ones. How often are you telling yourself that you don't look nice, you haven't got anything to offer in a meeting, you can't express yourself properly, you always make unfortunate choices? If your self-esteem is low, no doubt you are having these thoughts regularly, and, in stressful situations, you're hearing them shouting at you so much that you are incapacitated by the noise.

Learn to turn down the volume. These thoughts are not who you are, they are what you choose to tell yourself. Perhaps you didn't or don't get the support you need at home. Perhaps you're in a job that doesn't suit you. Whatever the reason for your discomfort and your inability to take control, positive thinking will go a long way to remedying the situation, because for every negative "What if" there is a positive one to take its place.

If you constantly focus on the negative then you will limit your ability to think realistically and creatively. You will express yourself negatively, your body language will follow suit, and other people will react to you negatively and possibly dismiss your comments and opinions.

   Aha! Moment

One negative thought has so much more weight than several positive ones!

You need to constantly remind yourself of your good qualities and what you've got going for you. Retrain your brain to concentrate on the positive, whatever it is. If, for example, you feel your writing skills are not quite up to the level of your colleagues', rather than tell yourself how inadequate you are, talk to yourself about how you are going to go about finding a course you can attend, and how you're going to convince the company to pay for it! Your body language will then change and you will start to give out more positive signals. We'd put money on you receiving more positive vibes in return as well.

 Try This

Here's a fun exercise we like to do in our workshops.

Write down:

Two physical attributes you like about yourself.

"I like my _____ and my _____."

Two qualities you like about your personality.

"I am _____ and _____."

One talent or skill that you like in yourself.

"I'm good at _____."

Remind yourself about these good points often, particularly when you feel low or nervous.

Once you are on the road to feeling better about yourself, you will be more willing to interact in a variety of ways with other people. This will certainly help you in your communication and your ability to develop strong, authentic business relationships.

 Aha! Moment

If I think more confidently and positively, I will be able to communicate more confidently and effectively, and will get people to co-operate with me more easily!

Other ways to develop better working relationships

1. Find common interests

The first step in helping people get to know you is to start getting to know others and finding out where your interests intersect. Too many of us wait for others to show an interest before we are willing to engage. When you make an effort to discover common interests and experiences, be it with colleagues or with clients, you can then build on these commonalities. For example, notice things on your colleague's desk — a photo or an interesting object from a holiday. Perhaps you'll also have story to share. Show an interest in the periodicals they are reading. Perhaps you'll learn something new that you can discuss. Ask them how they spent their weekend. Perhaps you can exchange restaurant recommendations.

2. Make others feel important

One of the most fundamental rules of developing relationships is to respect other people's feelings. This rule will make you many friends and enhance your reputation as a communicator. Everyone likes to be recognised and appreciated. If you can show this in the way you treat other people, you will reap many rewards.

Feeling unimportant is extremely de-motivating. If you have ever felt like the boss doesn't notice you, or worse still doesn't even know who you are, then you'll know what we're talking about. If you are a manager, make an effort to talk to your staff from time to time, and not always about business. Ask them about their families, their personal goals, their upcoming holiday. Listen to them. Show that you are approachable. By doing this you will win their respect and they will enjoy working for you. At the same time, you will learn more about your team and will pick up important information that will help you guide and motivate them.

3. Share some humour

Most of us gravitate toward people we can share a laugh with, as humour releases tension and adds glue to relationships. If we laugh at the same things, it means we have common feelings and perceptions, and we feel a sense of mutual understanding.

However, humour can also damage relationships. No doubt you have been dismayed upon discovering that a colleague or client finds something funny that you find distasteful, or have been embarrassed to find yourself laughing alone in a meeting. This danger is no reason to avoid humour, however. All you need to do is to stay on subjects that are safe to play around with.

As a basic rule of thumb, it is safe, to:	It is unsafe and highly questionable to:
• Make fun of yourself • Tell amusing stories about your family • Tell jokes that involve funny animals rather than people	• Make fun of people in the office • Tell jokes that show disrespect for gender, race, religion and political persuasion • Use crass language to get a laugh

People are very sensitive, and will often feel disinclined to tell you if they've been offended, so don't imagine that your coarse jokes are being appreciated simply because no one is complaining. Stick to the safe areas, and you will be successful.

4. Show humility

While we know that confidence is an attractive trait in a communicator, so indeed is humility. As we have discussed, arrogance is not confidence; it is in fact weakness. By the same token, humility is not weakness; it is strength. When you are truly confident, you will be humble enough to take responsibility for your errors in judgement and your missteps. You will know that we all have lots to learn at every step of the way through life, and this humility will keep you open to new information and experiences.

5. Be courteous

We find it astonishing how discourteous people can be in the office, and no doubt you do as well. These discourtesies range from not saying hello to colleagues in the morning to outright verbal abuse. When pressed, most people who behave this way will plead stress, saying that the pressures of work have made them distracted and irritable. They expect everyone to understand this, because, frankly, who isn't busy?

It's true; we're all busy. But being busy doesn't shut off our desire for, and our right to, a harmonious work environment. We all want and need to get our work done, and we can best do so when communication is founded on mutual respect. Discourtesies interrupt the flow of work, and lead to greater frustration rather than less. Your stress can stress the people around you, and the whole system can break down. Courtesy is the oil that keeps the engine of any relationship running smoothly.

Try This

If you find the spark is missing in your professional relationships, consider improving your listening skills and eye contact, since this behaviour evidences all the elements of communication described here. As you develop in these areas, you will notice how your conversations improve and your rapport with others builds. There's a lot on this in the next chapter!

You can learn much more about how to click with people from the moment you meet in Heather Hansen's book, *Powerful People Skills*.

The importance of timing

No matter how good you are at communicating, if you get your timing wrong, you don't stand much chance of obtaining the right results. Very often, success or failure will depend on choosing the right moment for a conversation.

Let's look at some bad times to communicate.

When the receiver is:

- pre-occupied or distracted

- in a hurry

- not feeling well

- in a bad mood

- highly emotional

- reading something or focusing on their computer screen

- continually interrupting

When the sender is:

- short of time to get the message across and receive feedback

- not sure of all the facts

- highly emotional

- unclear or confused about his/her stance on the issue

Other times to avoid are when:

- a phone call or visitor may interrupt

- there is ill feeling between the sender and receiver

- there are visual or aural distractions

With so much to consider, it's easy to see how communication can break down. However, there is so much to gain from considering all these issues and choosing just the right moment before you start to speak.

Star Tips for becoming a better communicator

1. Remember that first impressions aren't always the right impressions.

2. Be authentic. This involves understanding your own values, being sincere, and being genuine.

3. Be credible. This involves cultivating your knowledge and developing your relationships.

4. Be consistent. This creates trust.

5. Increase your confidence by having faith in your own ideas and being open to the ideas of others.

6. Focus on positive thoughts rather than negative ones. This will give your confidence — and therefore your communication skills — a helpful boost.

7. Learn to laugh at yourself. This is a major asset to any communicator.

8. Be courteous even under stress. This can make all the difference in professional, and personal, communication.

9. Practice humility. It's a strength, not a weakness.

10. Make sure you choose the right timing.

LISTENING

"Are you really listening… or are you just waiting for your turn to talk?"

Robert Montgomery

3

Why listen at all?

Without listening, communication doesn't occur. Good listening skills are the fundamental building blocks for everything else, so naturally they have a major impact on your effectiveness at work, as well as on the quality of your relationships.

We don't just listen to hear. There are lots of other reasons as well:

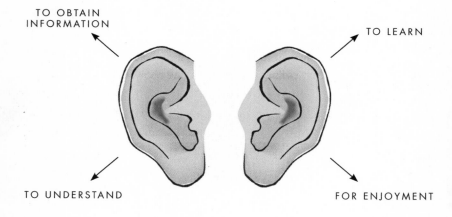

TO OBTAIN INFORMATION

TO LEARN

TO UNDERSTAND

FOR ENJOYMENT

Despite the importance of listening for personal and professional success, no one really teaches us how to do it, any more than they teach us how to breathe or walk. Listening is a skill that comes naturally, but not fully. Many studies reveal that we remember a dismal 25–50 per cent of what we hear. This means that when you talk to your boss, colleagues, customers or partner for 10 minutes, they generally only take in 2½–5 minutes of the conversation.

One thing is for certain though: It's hard to find a great leader who hasn't acquired good listening skills. The consequences of not listening carefully can be disastrous, so if you are aiming to climb the ladder of success, learning to listen must be your top priority. By improving your listening skills, you will increase your productivity, as well as your ability to influence, persuade, and negotiate. You will also avoid conflict and misunderstandings and encourage camaraderie and loyalty.

Obstacles to effective listening

Communicating would be fairly straightforward if our brains were clear enough to let us speak and listen simply and wholly. What makes it so complex and frustrating are the obstacles or barriers that get in the way. We have so many tasks requiring our attention — a list of duties a mile long, a head buzzing with dreams and schemes, plus of course all the stresses and strains of life in general. No wonder we sometimes find it difficult to pay attention long enough to listen. Effective listening involves temporarily putting all other thoughts on hold. Effective listening involves learning to manage what's going on in your mind.

In the previous chapters we discussed some of the bumps in the road to effective communication, including the different ways we perceive things, different interests, and emotions. Language and cultural barriers can be difficult to overcome too. We have also talked about how the location of the conversation — the environment, the noise level, and other distractions — can have an impact on communication in general, and on listening in particular.

Here are some other obstacles to effective listening that we regularly notice. Are you guilty of any of these? Take a moment to consider how these may make a listener feel, and the effect this will have on the success of the exchange.

- **Point-scoring.** You relate what you hear to your own experience in a game of oneupmanship, saying perhaps, *"Oh! That happened to me last week, only worse. Listen to this."*

- **Pseudo-listening.** You pretend to listen, while really you are listening to another conversation in the room, or thinking about something else.

- **Mind-reading.** You decide that you know what the other person is really thinking, perhaps saying to yourself, *"I bet that's not the real reason she did that."*

- **Preparing your next comment.** You are thinking about what you are going to say next, perhaps preparing a witty response, so you miss what the speaker is saying.

 Aha! Moment

Listening takes time. Whether or not I take this time can make or break my relationships.

Basic differences between a good listener and a bad listener

A bad listener	A good listener
is easily distracted	fights distractions
daydreams	makes an effort to focus
fakes attention	uses body language to show attention
tunes out dry subjects	considers the facts and data and asks, "What's in this for me?"
tunes out if delivery is poor	judges content over delivery
tends to challenge the speaker	interrupts only to clarify; gives speaker a chance
asks no questions	finds something in the content to engage with

How would you rate your listening skills?

Here are some questions to ask yourself to find out about your listening abilities. Answer these questions honestly, putting a tick beside any that you can say 'yes' to.

1. Do you tune out a speaker who is discussing a dry subject? ☐

2. Are you more conscious of a speaker's mannerisms than what they are saying? ☐

3. Do you fake attention to a person who's speaking? ☐

4. Do you find yourself mentally arguing with a speaker while they are still talking? ☐

5. Do you feel you can fill in the rest of a speaker's message after hearing just the first part?

6. When you have something on your mind, do you find it hard to concentrate on what the other person is saying?

7. Do you give up when the speaker is presenting hard-to-follow material?

8. When a speaker uses offensive language or says something you know to be untrue, do you have such a strong emotional reaction that you stop listening?

9. Do you allow your opinion of a speaker to influence your willingness to listen?

How many did you tick? If you ticked more than 6, then your listening skills leave a lot to be desired. Your poor listening skills may be affecting the way you relate to colleagues and friends.

 Aha! Moment

Listening is twice as hard as speaking. Fortunately I have two ears and only one mouth!

Four ways to listen

Most people listen in one of the following four ways:

Passive listening

Selective listening

Attentive listening

Active listening

We can of course switch between all these different methods, depending on what or whom we are listening to, but individuals tend to use one of these methods regularly. Let's look at these approaches in more detail. As we do, think about whether you can determine your usual listening method.

Passive listening

The passive listener provides very little verbal feedback to the speaker. Someone who is listening passively will:

- nod his/her head occasionally.

- give occasional verbal responses, such as "Really?" or "Uh huh."

- have a fairly expressionless look on his/her face.

- provide very little to stimulate the conversation.

It can be very frustrating talking to a passive listener, because you eventually wonder if the listener understands what you are saying, or even cares.

Selective listening

We've all heard the expression, "He hears what he wants to hear." This is the essence of selective listening. The selective listener is with you for part of the time, and then they tune out when they aren't really interested in what is being said. Someone who uses selective listening will:

- appear disinterested.

- glance at other things — a mobile phone, papers, people passing by.

- respond sharply when they hear something they feel strongly about.

- interrupt a speaker mid-sentence, and take over the conversation.

- change the topic of the conversation.

People listen selectively depending not only on the subject but also on the speaker. Imagine your boss coming up to you to give you some instructions. Chances are you'll pay attention. Now imagine that a boring or negative colleague comes along and rambles on and on about an office problem. Chances are that you'll tune him out straight away. This is selective listening.

Attentive listening

An attentive listener is more engaged in the conversation, and less judgemental. They concentrate more on the facts being provided in the message than on the emotional content. Attentive listeners will:

- show genuine facial expressions.

- use good eye contact with the speaker.

- nod occasionally to show understanding.

- provide regular verbal feedback ("I see," "Oh really?" "Uh huh") to encourage the speaker.

- ask questions to clarify the message.

- ask questions requiring more detail.

Attentive listeners do very well when the message is mainly factual. If the message involves emotions, this will prove difficult for an attentive listener. They can hear the message in the words, but they may not be able to fully understand the feelings.

Active listening

Active listening is also known as responsive or reflective listening. It is the most powerful form of listening. Active listeners take in the whole of the speaker's message and then confirm their understanding of the message. Active listeners capture not only the facts but the feelings as well. Active listeners will:

- show genuine facial expressions.

- use good eye contact and body language.

- nod occasionally to show understanding.

- encourage the speaker by providing verbal feedback.

- ask a balance of open and closed questions.

- show patience and empathy.

- show understanding of the message ("So you're saying that..." "I see, so the point is that...").

- acknowledge the emotions expressed with the message.

- explore reasons for the feelings being shown.

- listen to understand, not necessarily to agree or disagree.

Active listeners talk, but they make sure what they talk about is relevant to the speaker's message. Developing your active listening skills will without question have an impact on the quality of your communication.

Aha! Moment

How I listen conveys my attitude to the other person, and helps to make the exchange successful.

Listening to open doors

Doors talk, so make sure you listen. Only kidding! What we mean is, there are ways of listening that will open doors to communication with the person you are with, and there are ways that definitely keep them shut tight. Alison has a story to share about a way her son opened a door for her.

> I went in to my 11-year-old son's room to discuss something with him, and he was playing a game on his computer. I sat on his bed, next to his desk, and he turned to look at me as I spoke. After a brief moment he turned back to his computer and said, "I'll just shut off the monitor while you're talking." As we have had some issues about what he spends his time doing on his computer, I immediately said, "Why? What is it you don't want me to see?" He turned back to me with a look of surprise and disappointment. "You're welcome to see anything I'm doing," he said. "I just turned off the monitor because I know that it will distract me while you're talking, and I don't want to keep looking at it."
>
> I was overwhelmed by his maturity, and touched by this very unusual attention to what I was saying! His willingness to listen made it so much less frustrating to talk, and absolutely made my day.

Taking a few small actions, like silencing your phone or coming out from behind your desk when someone needs to speak with you, can make an enormous difference in the communication you have, reducing stress and putting feeling into the situation. Try it!

Keeping the doors open

In our workshops, before we go into detail about active listening skills, we often ask for two volunteers to pretend they are meeting for the first time. We appoint one person to ask questions and listen (Mandy) and the other to answer (Serene), then they introduce themselves.

Mandy: Hi. I'm Mandy.

Serene: Hi, I'm Serene.

Mandy: Where do you work?

Serene: ABC Technologies.

Mandy: What job do you do?

Serene: I'm a secretary.

Mandy: What do you do in your job?

Serene: Usual things, typing, administration work, filing.

Mandy: Do you enjoy your job?

Serene: It's OK.

Mandy: Oh.

Did you see what happened? Because of the lack of response from the listener, Serene didn't feel any compulsion to continue. She didn't even know if Mandy understood what was being said, or even cared about it. Mandy may also have been uninspired by Serene's answers, and was therefore listening selectively. It really takes two to do the conversational tango.

Now let's take a look at what normally happens after people have done some detailed work on improving listening skills. We're sure you'll spot the difference right away.

> Mandy: Hi Serene. What kind of company do you work in?
>
> Serene: *ABC Technologies — we are one of the largest providers of electronics and IT solutions in the region.*
>
> Mandy: Wow, that's great. And what do you do there?
>
> Serene: *I'm secretary to the Chief Financial Officer. I've been with the company for 8 years.*
>
> Mandy: What do you do in your job?
>
> Serene: *I assist the CFO in most of his duties.*
>
> Mandy: Oh, really? I do something similar. What's the scope of your job?

Serene: Well, it mostly involves dealing with his diary and appointments, making arrangements for meetings, taking minutes, liaising with directors and shareholders. My boss also gives me projects of my own to oversee.

Mandy: Wow! That's quite some responsibility. It sounds like you enjoy your job, and it's full of challenges.

Serene: Yes. My boss is very keen to involve me in the day-to-day running of the department. And how about you?

Look how much more communicating took place in this second conversation. What was the difference? Active listening played a big part. You can see that the listener, Mandy, was no longer just listening to the answers to simple questions; she was asking questions that gave her more information to listen to. When you have more information, you can ask better follow-up questions. Not only do you learn more about the person you are talking to, but they also feel respected and important, and will likely respond in kind. Doing anything else is really a waste of time!

 Fast Fact

A positive, detailed answer will usually lead to an in-depth discussion. Ask questions that will get you there.

Develop your door-opening skills

You can see that much of active listening actually involves talking, finding ways to open the doors to communication. Door-openers are like green lights for motorists. They are signals that listeners use to encourage speakers to elaborate on their message. Non-verbal door-openers can be very useful as they show the speaker that you are listening without interrupting. Verbal door-openers use one or two words that basically say to your listener, "Tell me more".

Non-verbal door-openers	Verbal door-openers
Offer a sincere smile	Right
Show a look of interest	I see
Turn and face the speaker	Really?
Lean toward the speaker slightly	Okay
Present a patient stance	Wow
Show a look of concern where appropriate	That's interesting
Nod your head to show you are following the message	Uh-huh

 Danger Zone

Beware of using the wrong non-verbal door-opener. A smile when the speaker is saying something very serious may be seen as a sarcastic sneer. It may show insincerity or a distracted mind, and will close doors rather than open them.

Aha! Moment

Sincerity is the key to ensure door-openers are effective.

Activate your active listening skills

Let's take your active listening skills a bit deeper, to make them as effective as possible.

Active listening is also known as empathetic listening; it is a technique counsellors often use because it puts the focus firmly on the person speaking. Active listening involves engaging with the speaker, encouraging the speaker to voice his/her views, and ensuring that you have really understood what was meant.

One of the key elements of active listening is paraphrasing the main points — restating the main essence of the speaker's message in your own words. This helps you, as a listener, to:

- show the speaker you are paying attention.

- reduce the possibility of misunderstanding.

- encourage the speaker to develop his/her message and feelings about it.

- be seen as empathetic, trying to understand, rather than challenge or contradict.

Myth Buster

If a speaker has a long message, it's important for me to keep interjecting. If I stay silent for too long, the speaker may think I'm not listening, and also my silence sometimes feels uncomfortable.

While we certainly recommend showing your engagement verbally with encouraging phrases, interjecting your own ideas can be dangerously close to taking over the conversation. Patience is one of the tools in the listening toolbox. It's much better to listen to the entire message rather than step on it before the speaker has finished.

Patience is particularly necessary on the phone, and it's important to be attentive not only to the words but also to the tone of voice in order to know when the speaker has finished a point.

Practice your paraphrasing

There are many useful phrases that you can use, which will act as cues to the speaker that you want to clarify your understanding. Let's look at some:

"I see. So what you're saying is..."

"What you're telling me is..."

"What I'm hearing you say is..."

"In other words..."

"So basically you feel that..."

When you use phrases like these and then put the speaker's message into your own words, there should be an inflection in your voice at the end. This indicates that you are questioning whether you've got it right. You could even add, "Is that correct?" thereby asking for confirmation in return.

Myth Buster

If I feel I have understood, then I have probably understood.

It's never a mistake to double-check. Too many things get in the way of understanding to risk making this assumption.

Fast Fact

Time is on your side! Thoughts move about four times as fast as speech.

Let's look at a few examples of how paraphrasing can be done.

Perhaps a colleague has said something like this in a meeting:

> "We've had so many frustrations in the development of our conference this year. First the committee couldn't come up with an appropriate theme, which pushed us back in the schedule. Then once the theme was decided, it was clear that there wasn't enough of a budget to achieve their extravagant goals. Now it's back in the committee again, and time is flying by."

If you want to emphasise the details of this situation, you might paraphrase like this:

> "I see. From what you're saying we've got both time and budget issues now. Does the committee have a deadline for when they have to get back to you about a new plan?"

In this way, you acknowledge what has been happening, and ask a question that can move the discussion forward, giving it some structure.

If, on the other hand, you think your colleague needs you to understand how he is feeling, you might say this:

> "So you're feeling really frustrated because you can't move into the planning stage, is that right?"

This will give him the validation and the opportunity to express himself fully. Once you've allowed this to happen, listening actively, you can then start brainstorming solutions to the problem.

Try This

Don't wait until you are in a critical situation to practice your active listening and paraphrasing skills. Try it when you're watching TV or reading the newspaper. Listen to an announcement, or read the first few paragraphs of an article, then paraphrase what you've learned. Polishing your skills in this way will help you when it comes to the real thing.

Star Tips for effective listening

1. Avoid prejudgement. Don't jump to conclusions because of the speaker's appearance, occupation or culture.

2. Appreciate the speaker's point of view and accept that it may not necessarily agree with yours.

3. Establish proper eye contact and give your full attention to the person speaking. This will help build both understanding and rapport.

4. Show that you are listening with your posture and the way you use your head, shoulders and limbs.

5. Don't interrupt. Let the speaker finish before you begin to talk, unless you need to clarify a point.

6. Look out for the main ideas. Listen specially for statements that begin with phrases such as "My point is..." or "The thing to remember is..." Listening out for key words or points will help to fix in your mind what is being said.

7. Paraphrase what someone has said, either to clarify the message or the feeling, to increase understanding and show empathy.

8. Respond verbally and non-verbally, so that the speaker knows you are engaged.

9. Reflect on what you have heard before responding.

10. Don't wait until the situation is critical. Start polishing your listening skills now!

SPEAKING —
THE MESSAGE ITSELF

*"Speech is human, silence is
divine, yet also brutish and
dead: therefore we must learn
both arts."*

Thomas Carlyle

4

Speaking to be understood

You've started working on your listening skills. Excellent. You will feel your conversations becoming richer and more effective right away. Now it's time to take a look at how you speak, so that you can make it easier for people to listen to you, and to understand you.

There's a huge difference between speaking and making yourself understood. No doubt you experience this from time to time as you go about your work. Haven't you left a conversation wondering, "What just happened?" or a meeting thinking, "What was her point?" People are always speaking, but this doesn't mean that they are always getting their point across.

How about you? Do you find that you have to repeat yourself to your colleagues because of frequent questions about your goals or procedure? When you talk to people, do their faces show understanding or confusion? Perhaps they need to develop their listening skills, but we all need to take responsibility for successful communication.

You don't just need to sound good; you need to make your message clear. In this chapter, therefore, we will be putting emphasis both on structure and on clarity in day-to-day business communication. We will also be looking at the words you use. We won't be looking at the subject of presentations and public speaking, as this is covered in Alison's book, *Present for Success*, also in the Success Skills series.

 Fast Fact

> Anything you can do to make yourself easier to understand will make your life easier, and diminish the tension that goes hand in hand with misunderstanding.

Clarity in your message

The first step in making your message clear is to make sure that you yourself understand it. The most efficient and most professional way to get your point across is to get it straight in your own mind before you express it to others on company time. Clarifying your message after the fact can take so much more time than reflecting on it sufficiently before you speak. Thinking things through might require some sort of sounding board. Alison says:

> When I was younger, I had a friend who was fantastic at telling me what I meant. When I had a big decision to make, he listened to me chatter on and on about how I felt, and then, when it was clear that I had come to the end of what I had to say, he took a moment and said something like, "Let me summarise: You're afraid it won't be worth the money." And he was usually absolutely right! It's wonderful to have a friend like that, who tells you what your message is.

It's perfectly appropriate to lean on friends to help you clarify what's important to you, or what's really bothering you. However, it's not as appropriate to expect colleagues or clients to be so interested and so understanding. The exception to this, of course, is when you are getting together to brainstorm. At such meetings you can feel free to let your ideas out as they come, putting lots of things on the table that can be clarified later. But in normal meetings it's best not only to have thought things through beforehand, but also to have decided on a structure for your thoughts.

 Aha! Moment

It's always best to get my message straight in my own mind before trying to communicate it to others.

Structuring your message

Not a lot of people think hard about structuring their message. They don't ask themselves things like, "What shall I start with? Do I need to ask any questions before I offer my thoughts? How will I link my two suggestions so they will be clear?" Of those who do think about it, many make their structural choices based on what they want to say. We can be much more effective, however, when we also consider our listeners and how best they will hear what we want to say. This is as true for a conversation at the coffee machine as it is in a board meeting.

Informal conversations

Let's look at a simple example. Imagine you need to talk to a colleague, Martin, about the fact that he listens to the radio while he's working in the cubicle next to yours. You've asked him several times to turn it down, but you find it distracting no matter the volume. You've decided you need to have a conversation about it, and the message you want to deliver is this: "I can't work with your radio on, so please turn it off." It's simple. It's clear. It's to the point. The danger is that it will sound like your main goal is to express your irritation rather than to find a solution. A bit more reflection on your colleague's character and the need to be on good terms with someone you see every day will give you some clues as to a more effective way to structure the conversation.

Have you thought of how you would deal with this? Take a look at an approach that we think could be very effective:

You choose not to interrupt Martin when he's working, and join him in the pantry when he goes to get a cup of coffee.

You: Hi Martin.

Martin: *Oh, hi.*

You: How's it going today?

Martin: *Good. Busy, as usual. I've got that presentation on Friday.*

You: Yes, I remember. Let me know if I can help.

Martin: *Thanks.*

You: Hey, while we're here, can I just ask, do you find the office noisy? Is that why you play the radio, to block out the noise?

Martin: *No, actually, I find it too quiet! I'm one of those people who need a bit of music to keep the creative juices flowing.*

You: Oh, I see. That's interesting. But the thing is, I'm one of those people who are very sensitive to noise, so I find the sound of your radio really distracting, and I want to find a solution that will suit both of us.

Martin: *Oh, I didn't know. I thought that turning it down helped.*

You: I hoped it would, but it didn't. So let's think of something else.

Martin: *Any ideas?*

You: I've got two, actually. One would be for you to wear earphones to listen to the music.

Martin: *And the other?*

You: Well, one of us could move to a different part of the office.

Martin: *That seems a bit dramatic.*

You: To me, too. I like working near you so we can talk. What do you think about earphones, then?

Martin: *Um, I could try. I don't want people to think they can't talk to me if I have the earphones on, though.*

You: I hadn't thought of that! Well, I could make a big show of talking to you and you could make a big show of not being irritated, and then people would know it was okay!

Martin: *Worth a try. I'll bring earphones tomorrow.*

You: Thanks so much. I really appreciate your willingness.

Let's break down the structure you chose for this conversation.

1. You didn't come right out with your message; you led up to it with a question about Martin and his frame of mind. Perhaps, if he had been in a very bad mood, you might have decided to wait for a better moment. As it was, he was just busy, as usual, but fine.

2. You offered to help, and this may have laid the groundwork for him to be helpful in return.

3. You opened the subject of your concern with a question, showing your desire to learn more about why he listens to the radio.

4. Once he explained, you told him your side of things. It's a very good structural choice to listen first, then talk, so that you know what you are dealing with in the moment.

5. Finally, you offered possible solutions to the problem — not just one, which might sound like an ultimatum, but two. This gave Martin a choice of solutions to consider, making him feel that he had a bit of control over the matter.

Can you see that part of the success of this structure is that it showed you had reflected, and that you cared? Too often, busy people merely express their stress rather than *manage* their stress.

 Danger Zone

Just because you have worked hard on communicating well doesn't mean that a conversation will necessarily go the way you hope it will.

We can't control how other people react, but we can quite easily increase our chances that the conversation will go well by preparing for it in advance. If it doesn't go well, at least you know that you gave it your best shot.

Formal situations

In a more formal setting, not structuring your communication can spell even bigger disasters than some bad feelings between a few colleagues. When you ramble in meetings you waste people's time, and the same goes for when you are dull and monotonous. Speaking too simply, imagining that everyone knows what you mean, can also be a big problem. All of these tendencies are likely to lead your colleagues or clients to make some negative decisions about their desire to work closely with you in the future.

It will always pay you back in spades to reflect not only on your message but also on who your listeners are. Thinking about your audience will help you decide how to introduce your message, and how to link your main points to their point of view. Here's an example to help you understand what we mean.

Imagine you have to motivate your team to improve their sales figures. You've been pushing them, but nothing seems to have changed. You can see they are working hard, but that they don't feel hopeful. So your basic message is that they've got to work in a new way to remedy the situation. Are you simply going to get them together and say, "Okay folks, the way you work isn't successful. You've got to try a new way. Things are really tough out there, so hurry up and do it"? I hope not, although this is in fact how some people choose to communicate.

Reflect a bit. You know they are working hard. Their effort isn't an issue; it's the approach that is unsuccessful. Clearly they haven't thought of a new one, so it will take some brainstorming to come up with a strategy you can trust. Do people embrace change right away, even if what they are doing doesn't work? Not usually. So it will make sense for you to lead up to your message with language that will make your team feel encouraged rather than criticised. You might say something like this:

> *"It's tough out there, isn't it? It's getting more and more competitive, and in these times we have fewer resources than usual. I can see you are all working very hard to make the numbers, and I appreciate that so much. Sales aren't improving, however, and we're all going to be discouraged and unmotivated soon, if we aren't already. I'd like to suggest that we take some time, perhaps half a day, to push the day-to-day requirements of work aside, and share our experiences and ideas. I'd like our goal to be a sense of clarity on what's working and what isn't, as well as the development of a strategy for eliminating wasted time and energy."*

You didn't start with, "It's not working." You started with empathy. As we discussed in the previous chapter, empathy is the hallmark of a good listener. It is equally a sure sign of a good speaker. Put yourself in your listener's or listeners' shoes, consider their point of view, and you will be able to structure your message in a win-win way.

Fast Fact

Another clear, sensitive, and therefore effective way of structuring your communication, particularly for difficult conversations, is called the 3 F's. This is laid out for you in Chapter 6, where we talk about assertiveness.

Danger Zone

Beware of giving clarity such a high priority that you omit all emotion from the way you speak.

In the beginning was the word, and the word was easy to misunderstand (aka Choose your words with care)

You can see how much emphasis we have already put on considering who your communication partners are, and choosing language that suits them. It's obviously very important to avoid jargon that your listener is unfamiliar with, unless you intend to teach it to them during the conversation. There are also quite a few words we all use but don't realise are undermining our relationships. Let's take a look at some words that generate negative perceptions and reactions.

1. Always

'Always' and 'never' are two words that you should always try never to use. It's a funny way to put it, isn't it? But it's really true, above all when we are talking about the way people behave. It's fine to say something like, "Please always put your completed invoices in my in-tray, so I can find them easily," since you're discussing an operating procedure. However, when you say, "You always do such a rush job on the invoices and they're always really sloppy," it's a bit more problematic. First of all, if the person you are talking to can point to an example or two of an invoice that wasn't at all sloppy, you have to take your words back and start again. Also, a word like 'always' can easily be perceived as an attack on the listener. When you consider that you are really trying to improve the situation by having this conversation in the first place, it is much better to choose a softer approach, looking for a win-win solution, as you did with Martin and his radio music.

2. Never

'Never' is similar to 'always'. Saying to someone, "You never come to work on time!" will never (oops!) be as effective as taking the tardy employee aside and saying something like, "I've noticed you've not been getting to work on time quite a lot lately. Are you having trouble getting out of the house in the morning?" They won't feel attacked, and you can take the conversation from there.

3. Should

A huge pitfall for many people is the use of 'should'. The word 'should' too easily indicates criticism and disapproval. Again, when used with standard operating procedures, it's not a problem; you are not in danger when you say, "You should always replace the paper in the copy machine if it runs out when you are using it." However, when you say, "You should spend more time proofreading your work," it can come across as quite harsh, unless it is your answer to the question, "What should I do?" Even when people ask us what they should do, it's still a nice approach to avoid giving them a concrete answer, and instead to tell them what they "might try" or what you "would like to suggest." Because, in the end, you probably don't know what's right for them. Give them your ideas, but don't lay down the law.

When we use 'should' in the past tense, it can be very unhelpful as well. If you come into a meeting with your boss after getting drenched in a rain shower and she immediately says, "You should have carried an umbrella with you," how does it feel? You have already come to that conclusion yourself, haven't you? You're already soaking and embarrassed; no such comments are necessary! It would be much more helpful to focus on the moment, rather than the past. It would be lovely if she said, "Would you like to take a moment to dry off before we start?" or "Shall we see if anyone has a spare jacket in the office?" Anything we can do to offer tangible help to someone, rather than merely point out the obvious, will lead to greater trust and appreciation all around.

4. But

The word 'but' can be seen as a negative word. It can feel as if it erases everything positive that came before it. The listener therefore focuses on the negative. Compare these two sentences:

> *"This model is very popular but it only does 35 miles per gallon."*

> *"This model is very popular and it does 35 miles per gallon."*

You can immediately see how positive the second sentence sounds, and how there is no change in the information, only in the attitude. We are not saying you must always avoid using 'but'; just be aware of its negative implications and do consider if an alternative may be appropriate.

5. Weak words

'Try', 'maybe', 'perhaps' — these are weak or wimpy words. They don't imply any sense of commitment, only uncertainty. "I'll try to work on that tomorrow" gives you an excuse in case you don't get round to working on it. ("Oh well, I tried, but it didn't work.") Or what about, "Maybe I'll come to your place tomorrow afternoon." That will leave me wondering if I should stay home and prepare tea. Avoid using words like these that weaken your message.

6. Unnecessary phrases

Often known as trigger phrases, these are unnecessary as they add no real meaning to your message. They are the sort of phrases that turn off your listener as soon as they hear them, so they don't even want to stick around for the actual message. Here are some trigger phrases:

"You know what I mean." (Are you telling me you're not sure if you've explained yourself very well?)

"To be quite honest with you…" (Were you being dishonest before then?)

"Please don't take this personally…" (So you're about to offend me, yes?)

"Now don't take this the wrong way." (I'm definitely going to take it the wrong way.)

7. Demanding phrases

Phrases like "You have to…", "You must…", "You'd better… or else" are very demanding, and they make people feel like they have no choice.

8. Demeaning words

Words like 'stupid', 'idiot' and 'jerk' are hurtful, discouraging and unkind. They are evidence of your emotions getting the better of you.

9. Negative words

'No', 'can't', 'don't' and other negative words shut down discussions and stir up negative feelings. It's best to avoid them where possible. Ask yourself if you are using them because you are unwilling to consider other points of view, and find ways to stay open.

You want the people you are communicating with to keep listening, and to keep making an effort to understand your message. When we use dangerous words and phrases as discussed here, we run the risk of having people take a step away from the conversation, if only inside their own heads.

Aha! Moment

Even if I'm trying to be helpful, it's best to be sensitive to how different words and phrases will come across to the listener.

Magic words to use often

People will feel better towards you if you communicate courteously. Here are some very significant words and phrases in the English language. Use them often. Just like your mothers told you to.

Please	Would you mind?
I'm sorry	What are your thoughts?
Unfortunately	May I?
Thank you	Excuse me
You're welcome	I understand

Try This

Consider these words and ask yourself how you would use them appropriately and how they may be used in a dangerous way:

You didn't	You'd better
You have to	I insist
That can't be true	Surely not

Star Tips for planning a well-structured and effective message

1. Have a clear goal in mind before trying to communicate your message to others.

2. Reflect on an appropriate structure for your message before delivering it.

3. Plan effectively so that you reduce time wasted in misunderstanding.

4. Choose the right moment for a conversation so that you increase the likelihood that the communication will be successful.

5. Use empathy to build rapport and be more persuasive.

6. Listen first, then speak!

7. Be aware of the fact that generalisations (such as the use of 'always' and 'never') can come across as insulting.

8. Avoid weak words and phrases to make sure your message is motivating.

9. Be sensitive to how different words will be received by your listeners.

10. Don't undermine relationships and turn people off by using the wrong words.

SPEAKING — IT'S NOT JUST WHAT YOU SAY, IT'S ALSO HOW YOU SAY IT!

"We often refuse to accept an idea merely because the tone of voice in which it has been expressed is unsympathetic to us."

Friedrich Nietzche

5

Vocal clarity

Even if you have clarified your message to yourself and have used empathy to develop your approach, the way you say the words can muddy your message. Both the way you pronounce the words and the tone of voice you use will have an effect. So just as using the right words is essential, it's important to make an effort to use an effective tone. Your voice, your face and your body all have a role to play in how you are understood.

You say potato, I say potahto

Pronunciation will be more of an issue in a multicultural environment than in a homogeneous one. Those of you who work for multinational companies will be familiar with how often one can end up wondering, "Did he say 'thought' or 'taught'? Was that word 'pilot' or 'pirate'? Did she really say 'sheet', or was it something else?!"

Shirley has a very relevant personal experience to share about this:

> When I first came to Singapore from Sheffield in 1983, my employer and colleagues had quite a challenge understanding my Yorkshire accent. My students had an even greater challenge. I remember one day saying to a class, "Oooh I'm eatin' some very different food since I've been in Singapore. Last night, me friends took me out and it's the first time I've ever eaten duck." Now in Yorkshire, we pronounce the word 'duck' the same as the word 'book'. I would also use this deep 'oo' sound in words like 'love', 'up', 'under', 'cup'. So having told my students that I had eaten duck, one girl looked at me and said, "You ate a dog?" Obviously the way I said the word 'duck' sounded to her like 'dog'. After having a laugh with the students, they all started trying my Yorkshire accent, which had everyone in stitches. I knew then that to avoid misunderstandings, I was the one

who had to take responsibility for increasing the clarity of my speech. I couldn't expect an entire nation to change, after all. So I quickly realised that I had to speak more slowly, pronounce my words more clearly, especially the beginnings and the endings, and take particular care with words containing 'u'. It took me a while, but I learned that when I smile broadly I can say 'up', 'under', 'cup', 'love', 'but', 'butter', 'duck', etc in exactly the same way that Singaporeans do. The only problem is that after a while my face starts to ache!!

Fast Fact

You can read another funny story about Shirley's first overseas posting on page 156.

Four steps to increasing vocal clarity

Fortunately, Shirley was able to make the required adjustments to her accent. But what if you find it extremely difficult to do this, because your accent is so strong? This simple four-step process will help you right away.

Step 1:	**Slow down.** We can often understand words individually that we would have trouble picking out of a rapid sentence.
Step 2:	**Keep your language simple.** Let people slowly get used to the way you speak.
Step 3:	**Check for understanding.** Ask your listeners if they have understood your pronunciation, since they may hesitate to tell you themselves.
Step 4:	**Make use of written messages.** Do this either as an introduction to a spoken conversation, or as a follow-up afterwards, to make sure your meaning is clear.

People from the same culture can also have trouble understanding each other, especially when a speaker is prone to mumble or to speak as if they need to dash off to catch a train. If you are aware that you are guilty of either of these tendencies, there's a very clear-cut solution:

e-nun-ci-ate

Take the time to enunciate (or articulate) clearly, and you won't have to take more time to repeat yourself. It may feel a bit (or very) unnatural to you at first, as it's not your normal way of speaking, but stick with it. Your comfort level will rise, and more importantly, your clarity will improve, which means your listener's comfort level will increase. As a result, your conversations will be more productive and your reputation will be enhanced.

 Aha! Moment

The more I learn to enunciate words carefully, the more effective my message will be.

Touch up your tone

Remember when you were a child and your parents used to say to you, "Don't you use that tone of voice with me, young lady," or "I don't think I appreciate that tone, young man"? Your tone may have very authentically represented how you were feeling, but it clearly wasn't appropriate to the situation (at least in your parents' opinion!) and it wasn't helping to resolve things.

Well, tone is equally important now that we're all grown up. Even more than the words being said, our tone provides listeners with clues to so many things, including whether or not the speaker believes in what he/she is saying, whether or not the speaker is enthusiastic, and whether or not we need to feel threatened in the situation.

Since it's part of our survival skills to pick up these signals, most people can hear the variations in a speaker's tone when they are listening. We generally tune out both monotonous and overly noisy speakers; we generally enjoy conversing with people who vary their tone depending on what they are saying and to whom; we generally avoid as much as possible people who express a lot of irritation when they speak to us.

Myth Buster

Well-chosen words speak for themselves.

Only if people are still listening! Choose tones that listeners will want to listen to.

Given how sensitive we are to the sound of others, it's strange how many of us are deaf to the effect our own tone has. Some people may find a monotonous voice as stupefying as everyone else does, but when it comes to their turn to speak, they may be just as monotonous. We don't want to listen to it, but we don't hear it in ourselves. (Or we do hear it, but don't want to make the effort to change it.) Similarly, we may have the normal reaction of recoiling or digging in our heels when someone speaks to us sharply. But when we are irritated and want things to change, we may speak just as sharply, and bizarrely end up surprised when nothing changes.

Try This

Work on the range of tones at your disposal by practicing saying the same thing in different ways. For example, say "I'm very happy to see you" first with a neutral, monotonous tone. Do you sound convincing? Now say it in an overly enthusiastic way. How does that sound? What if you say it as if you're thinking about something really irritating that happened earlier in the day? Will any of these tones work when you really want to convince someone of your sincerity? Start being aware of the tones you use at work, and consider whether they are the ones that best suit your purpose.

Emotional excess

Emotions very often keep people from communicating. They may be too scared, or too territorial, or too proud. You have probably also noticed that emotions force people to communicate too quickly, or too aggressively, or inconclusively, or incoherently. Why is this? Well, when we get emotional, we experience a surge of the chemical adrenalin in our bodies. This happens whether we are angry, delighted, or ashamed. High levels of adrenalin limit our ability to think rationally. We need to calm ourselves to lower the adrenalin before we can think. Once we can think, we can trust ourselves to talk.

If you feel very emotional about something, it may be better to wait for a while before trying to put the message across. Communication can often fail if we are highly charged about an issue, and equally if the person speaking to us is highly charged. Just as you can ask for a moment to calm down and get your thoughts together before continuing an emotional discussion, you can ask someone who is getting emotional to take a moment and do the same. This can be done respectfully, so as not to inflame things further, by telling them that you want the discussion to be as productive as possible, and so that no one says something they will later regret.

Danger Zone

Don't imagine that it's part of being authentic to show when you are angry.

Showing when we're angry may be authentic, but this doesn't mean that we should trust ourselves to speak at these times, especially in professional situations.

As the writer Ambrose Bierce put it, "Speak when you are angry and you will make the best speech you will ever regret." Take time to calm down, and make sure you understand the situation. Choose your words. Choose your tone. Then open your mouth.

It really pays to consider your tone of voice when you do business. It is imperative for face-to-face communication. Tone is even more important over the phone, because a lot of energy is lost over the phone lines and you don't have the benefit of eye contact or body language. This means you need even more energy on the phone than you do face to face.

Vocal hazards

Your voice can be your greatest tool in your communication toolbox, but the way you use it can prevent you from being understood in the best possible way. Here are some hazards to watch out for.

1. Being too loud

If your volume is turned up too high, you may sound aggressive rather than assertive. This will come across as overpowering and perhaps intimidating.

2. Being too soft

On the other side of the coin are people who speak very softly. Just as we don't want to listen to a person who shouts, we also don't listen to people who speak too softly. Speaking softly comes across as lacking confidence, and it will not help you deliver your message effectively.

3. Mumbling

Mumbling may be part of being soft spoken, or it could also be a confidence issue. If people keep asking you to repeat yourself because of your mumbling, this will become very frustrating, and it will detract from presenting a clear, confident message.

4. Sounding uncertain

Nerves may be to blame if your voice sounds shaky or hesitant, or it could be that you're not sure of your message. If you sound uncertain, how can you expect other people to have confidence in what you are saying?

5. Questioning tone

Uncertain people sometimes raise their voice at the end of each sentence, as if asking questions all the time. Imagine these statements sounding like questions: "My name is John Lim?", "We're going to have a great day today?" It's impossible to come across as mature or authoritative when you speak this way.

6. Condescending tone

One to be avoided at all costs is the "I'm better than you" tone in your voice. A patronising, condescending tone will very quickly get the other person's back up and do nothing for developing relationships.

7. Bluntness

Negative situations happen in life. It's unfortunate, but it's true. When associated emotions are reflected in your message, however, it can sound much worse than you intended. For example, frustration can sound like an angry accusation. Directness can be received as rudeness and people may take offence. Offended people stop listening.

The key to getting your vocal expression right is to learn to manage your emotions and be sincere. People will find what you say worth listening to and they will see you in a positive light.

 Try This

Find a friend to help you with this. Prepare a short message of two or three sentences. Deliver it first of all in a very blunt, direct way, holding nothing back. Then repeat the message in a concerned, assertive tone.

How did the other person respond? What has it taught you about your vocal expression?

Facial clarity

Did you notice that when you tried the last exercise, you changed your facial expression dramatically in order to produce the required effect? It's practically impossible for a human to produce a happy sound without putting on a happy face, or to sound angry without looking angry. When we try to sound neutral, our faces also go blank. As a result, our facial expressions play a big role in delivering our meaning, and can also kill our meaning completely. A moment's thought can make all the difference, as Alison explains:

> I was consulting in a company that was experiencing a lot of misunderstandings, the most serious of which were between the CEO, a man, and the VP of marketing, a woman. The VP felt ill at ease because the CEO seemed very cold and critical to her. I had trouble understanding this at first, because he seemed quite open and understanding to me. And indeed he was. But he regularly looked at her, or anyone who walked in his office, with what I now refer to as Work Face. This is the face we put on when we are working hard, thinking, concentrating, digging for solutions. When someone knocks at our door and we look up at them, we still have Work Face on. All it really means is that we are still concentrating, but to the person who just knocked, it looks for all the world like, "What the heck do you want?" and has a very inhibiting effect.
>
> When I first saw the CEO's Work Face, I recognised what the VP had been worrying about. So I explained to her that she needn't take his look personally at all. I also suggested to him that he take a moment to relax and adopt an open facial expression when a colleague knocked at his door, so he made sure they felt comfortable talking to him. If they stopped talking, he'd have a lot more trouble running the company!

Do you tend to look at people wearing your Work Face? Try relaxing your face when someone approaches you; you'll see what can happen if you make an effort to be more welcoming.

What is your body saying?

Okay, so now you've worked on structuring your message, you've considered it from your listener's point of view, you're enunciating clearly, you've chosen an appropriate tone and you've sorted out your face. Are you done? Nope! Sorry! Speaking is an activity that is most effective when not only your face but also your body supports your message.

Take a look at the following three illustrations. The speaker is using the same words, but is using her face and her body in three different ways. Which one do you think would put the applicant most at ease?

"You're clearly very well-qualified for this job. I'm glad you applied."

No doubt you answered that the third illustration shows a woman whose body language and facial expression both support her words. Naturally, if her goal is in fact to make this applicant feel uncomfortable, one of the other attitudes would suit her goals better. But if your objective is to gain people's trust and be convincing, make sure that your body language isn't the enemy of your words.

Body language bloopers

You want your posture, gestures and facial expressions to support your message, and help you appear confident and relaxed. There are certain behaviours that will not work in your favour, however. Here are some to be aware of.

1. Slouching

Some big comfortable chairs are very easy to slouch in; you just want to lean back and relax. When you do this, though, the danger is looking too relaxed and informal. People might not take you seriously, and, just as importantly, might not think you take them seriously either. Just as your mother taught you at the dining table, it's best to sit up — and stand up — straight if you want to come across as an assertive, confident communicator.

2. Distracting habits

Do you twist your hair, or play with your rings? Do you click your pen continuously, or twirl it around? Such distractions will ensure the listener is paying attention to your habits, and forming judgements about them, instead of concentrating on your message.

3. Invading space

Have you ever been in conversation with someone who keeps getting closer and closer, too close for comfort, and often quite loud too? You end up leaning away from them and feeling very uncomfortable. There is no hard and fast rule as far as safe space is concerned, but no one feels comfortable when the other person is insensitive to personal space.

4. Hovering

It's uncomfortable to talk to someone who is standing over you while you sit. For maximum comfort, try to be on the same physical level, especially if the conversation is more than a couple of minutes long. If both people are seated, there will be little disparity between levels, no matter how tall or short each person is.

5. Blank looks

The only time you want a blank look is when you are playing poker. When you are trying to convey an important message, it won't help you at all. Blank looks make you appear indifferent, and others will soon feel that way too. Put some expression in your face when you pass on as well as when you receive a message.

6. Harsh looks

It's never nice to talk to people who are frowning or scowling with their eyebrows all furrowed. They look rather unappealing and unapproachable. Such expressions also have a tendency to make the speaker's tone of voice rather sharp. Be aware of what your face is doing when you communicate.

7. Threatening gestures

Finger pointing and fist pounding are very strong messages and come across as aggressive and intimidating. This is not the sort of thing to do if you want to be known as a relaxed, positive, confident communicator.

 Aha! Moment

My face and body are important tools in my communication toolbox. I must use them to help me come across as a confident, relaxed communicator.

Do I look communicative in this?

Just as with your tone of voice and facial expressions, the first step to developing helpful body language is to develop an awareness of how you use your body when you are communicating. As you go through your day, ask yourself questions like these:

- Am I slouching? Does this project a lack of confidence?

- Do I fiddle with my rings during conversations? Might people think my mind is not focussed on what we're saying?

- Do I turn my body at an angle when people approach me, or do I open my body to them? Which way is more welcoming?

- Do I keep my head tilted back and look down my nose when I'm speaking? What might this mean to the listener?

- How often do I point an index finger at the other person's chest? Could this feel aggressive?

We're not saying that it is wrong to do any of these things. There can easily be times when you actually will want to use such behaviour in your communication. What we are saying, however, is that it is best for you to choose your body language rather than let your body choose for you. You may in fact be very distracted or irritated in a conversation, and want to fiddle with your rings, but before you go ahead and do so, ask yourself if this will serve the bigger purpose of getting the communication right and keeping emotions from calling the shots.

Once you are aware of how your body has been behaving while you weren't paying attention, you can start making minor adjustments that will lead to a big improvement in communication for you. Work on standing up a bit straighter, on tipping your head toward people you are talking to, on calming your hands. Think about the body language other people are using around you, and consider which positions and actions you appreciate when they are used with you. Then you can do the same with others.

Fast Fact

We learn to speak by imitation. We can improve the way we speak by continuing to imitate, until we've found something that works best for us.

As you can see, we have a wonderful variety of tools at our disposal both for giving and for receiving messages. Ensuring that you use as many of these tools as possible, improving as you go along, will pave the road to greater understanding and better relationships at work, both of which are essential for success.

Star Tips for using the right tone and body language

1. Enunciate as clearly as possible. Pronunciation differs greatly, not only between countries but also within them, so clear articulation helps.

2. Don't weaken your message by using the right words but the wrong tone. Your tone often determines whether your listeners are open to you, or closed.

3. Make sure your face matches your words. People will look into your eyes to see how genuine you are.

4. Be sincere when speaking, and people will find you worth listening to.

5. Be aware of what your body is saying when you speak. Your posture is very often determined by your emotional state.

6. Beware of body language bloopers, which will work against you in passing on your message.

7. Wait a while before speaking if you are highly emotional about an issue.

8. Evaluate your vocal clarity occasionally, and make appropriate adjustments.

9. Remember the key steps to increasing effectiveness: slow down, use simple language and check for understanding.

10. Follow up important conversations by sending an e-mail that restates the conclusions drawn.

ASSERTIVENESS AND YOU

*"A 'no' uttered from
the deepest conviction
is better and greater
than a 'yes' merely
uttered to please, or
what is worse, to avoid
trouble."*

Mahatma Gandhi

6

It's difficult to strike the right balance between putting our ideas across and accepting those of others, isn't it? A lot of us have trouble sticking up for ourselves, while many others insist on sticking up only for themselves. Somewhere in between lies the way to keep communication flowing for maximum efficiency and satisfaction.

What's your type?

There are dozens of ways to divide human personality traits and behaviour. Chances are you've heard of several of them, and perhaps you've looked into the details yourself. Doing so is very instructive, and can help you understand what makes the people around you tick, and communicate better with them as a result.

For the purposes of our discussion of day-to-day business communication, we find it very helpful to break behaviour down into four basic types as these are the ones that most dramatically affect communication flow:

Passive

Aggressive

Passive-aggressive

Assertive

It will help if you can recognise these types in both yourself and other people. Look through this table, and ask yourself to what extent the description applies to you. Highlight the main traits you recognise in yourself. Put a circle around the ones you would like to exhibit more.

Behaviour type	Body language	Traits
Passive Avoids confrontation. Doesn't stand up for his/her rights. Concerned about what people think of him/her.	Minimal eye contact. Quiet, uncertain voice. Defensive posture. Fidgets a lot.	Gives in easily. Beats around the bush. Does not express needs. Does not express rights. Doesn't achieve potential.
Aggressive Wants to win, even at expense of others. No respect for others' needs and rights.	Excessive eye contact. Strong, loud voice. Expansive posture. Invades others' space.	Quick to blame others. Very critical. Likes to interrupt. Appears authoritarian. Uses sarcasm to win a point. Requests sound like orders. Escalates situations easily. People get annoyed or intimidated and avoid contact.
Passive-aggressive A mix of passive and aggressive behaviour. Keen to get even while avoiding confrontation. Wants to assert him/herself but feels a lack of power to do so.	Minimal eye contact. Impatient sighs. Tight-lipped. Looks 'wound up'. Expression says "I don't believe it." Closed posture.	Indirect responses. Cutting humour and 'slips of the tongue'. Catty comments. Doesn't gain trust.

Behaviour type	Body language	Traits
Assertive Expresses needs. Defends rights. Respects self as well as others' needs and rights.	Good eye contact, but not uncomfortable. Moderate, even tone of voice. Body language to suit the words spoken.	Listens a lot. Seeks to understand. Treats everyone with respect. Aims for solutions. Direct without being abrupt. States clearly what he/she wants. Achieves results. Gains respect and affection.

Most people exhibit a mix of different types of behaviour, so these traits won't necessarily match you or the people you know in all respects. Also, we want to emphasise that there are certainly times when it pays to take a passive stance, and others when it can be best to take a more aggressive position. However, we can say that of the four types of behaviour in the table, there is only one that is designed to promote win-win situations as much as is humanly possible: the assertive type.

Fast Fact

Being assertive means communicating what you really want in a clear way, respecting your own rights and feelings as well as the rights and feelings of others. Assertiveness is an honest and appropriate expression of one's feelings, opinions and needs.

Myth Buster

Assertiveness is often seen as aggressive.

Putting your ideas forward assertively is, by definition, not aggressive. When you get the feedback that you are being aggressive, consider whether or not you have been respectful in your communication. Also consider whether the other person really wants to hear what you have to say.

Risks and costs of each behavioural type

A natural question to ask is, "If assertiveness is so effective, why doesn't everyone behave this way?" The answer is of course that many, many impulses underlie our behavioural choices.

Aggressive behaviour

In aggressive behaviour, it seems that the costs should be obvious. The lack of co-operation that results from aggression leads to conflict and a loss of respect and friendship. As a result, it can easily produce the opposite of the desired result. But still people behave aggressively. Why? For one, perhaps doing so has helped them achieve their goals in the past. They need to be shown that it won't work so well in the present. Aggressive behaviour is also linked to a desire for power and control, both of which are linked not with confidence but rather with insecurity. Very often, our insecurities speak to us more loudly than reason, and we risk relationships in order to satisfy them. Watch out for allowing your fears to make your decisions for you, when rational analysis will serve you much more loyally.

Passive behaviour

What's behind passivity, then? Most people are hired because of the perceived contribution they can make to an organisation, so if your behaviour is consistently passive, you are putting yourself at risk. It's very hard to promote people who don't promote themselves, so while keeping quiet may seem quite safe, it can actually be dangerous. People persist in this form of behaviour for many reasons, including: to avoid conflict; to be considered polite; to maintain others' approval; and to avoid having to deal with a strong reaction.

Passive-aggressive behaviour

Being passive-aggressive involves indirect resistance. Passive-aggressive people avoid confrontation, but seek to have an effect. For example, in order not to have to deal with an issue, they might misplace important papers. Rather than saying clearly how they feel about a subject, they might pout in order to make their attitude known but avoid putting words to the feeling. As with both aggressive and passive behaviour, passive-aggressive choices may feel successful in the short term, but they generally damage one's reputation. They seem to work quite nicely for children, but have no place in professional adult communication.

Assertive behaviour

Assertive behaviour, by design, seeks win-win solutions. Assertiveness depends on confidence, and only truly confident people are willing to listen to the ideas of others. Confident people know they can handle the communication that results when they offer their ideas. Assertiveness requires the ability to be forceful, but also the ability to listen.

Of course, assertiveness isn't the golden key that will open all doors. There are times when it will be the right choice to be passive. Perhaps you aren't yet clear enough on what is being discussed to offer an opinion, or perhaps people are reacting emotionally and you take a back seat until things calm down so as not to make the situation worse. At other times, being aggressive will serve you best. This could happen in a meeting you are leading, when no one seems to have understood the gravity of a situation, and no one is listening. You might choose to raise your voice a little and take control at this time. Or maybe there's someone in your office who behaves aggressively, and reasoning with him has had no effect. Directing aggressive behaviour at him might force him to reconsider his position. Our point is that communication requires a lot of tools, and it will help you enormously to be versatile. (It's very hard to find a 'right' time for passive-aggressive behaviour, however.)

How assertive are you?

Here are some questions to ask yourself to find out how assertive you are. Answer these questions honestly. Put a tick beside any that you can say 'yes' to.

1. Do you ask for help without feeling embarrassed? ☐

2. Do you ask questions when you're confused? ☐

3. Do you give praise to colleagues where praise is due? ☐

4. Are you able to say 'no' to a request without feeling guilty? ☐

5. Can you accept when others say 'no' to a request from you? ☐

6. Are you open and honest with your manager about difficulties you are facing? ☐

7. Do you volunteer opinions when you think or feel differently from others? ☐

8. Are you able to speak up in class or meetings? ☐

9. Do you speak with a confident manner, communicating caring and strength? ☐

10. Do you look at people when you're talking to them? ☐

11. If you want something, can you ask for it in a direct way? ☐

12. When making a complaint about service, do you state your case without aggression? ☐

How many did you tick? If you didn't tick at least 9, then you probably need to do some work in order to be more consistent in your assertive behaviour.

 Aha! Moment

When I'm assertive, everyone benefits.

Basic behaviour for assertiveness

Communicating assertively will help you to deal with many situations both at home and at work. By communicating assertively you are less likely to misunderstand or be misunderstood. The objective is not to get your own way all the time, but to try to reach a mutually agreeable outcome. Here are some rules to remember if you want to improve your assertiveness:

1. Use 'I' statements, like "I think," "I prefer," "I feel." "I" statements deliver a clean, clear statement of your side of things. For example:

   "When you have to rearrange appointments, I become very disorganised. I'd like to be notified as soon as possible please."

   "When you scold me in front of others, I feel very embarrassed. I'd prefer it if we could talk in your office in future."

Other examples:

"I appreciate your help on this because..."

"I think we'd benefit from..."

2. Offer suggestions rather than instructing, so that the other person can make up their own mind. For example:

    "Would it be practical to...?"

    "What do you feel about doing it this way?"

3. Ask questions to find out the thoughts, opinions and wishes of others.

    "I have some ideas for how to go about this process, but I want to make sure I hear yours as well."

4. Open a discussion to find solutions, with questions such as "How can we resolve this?" or "Why don't we give everyone a chance to offer an idea?"

5. Speak confidently without filler words and hesitant phrases like "er," "you know," and "well."

6. Use a steady tone of voice, speaking clearly and not too fast.

7. Keep a relaxed, upright posture.

8. If you don't have an answer, just say so and offer to find out. Don't bluff.

Danger Zone

It's important to avoid sounding provocative or critical. Using 'you' language, where the emphasis is placed on another's behaviour rather than on how you feel, can lead to inflamed feelings.

Learn to use 'I' language as much as possible, taking responsibility for the situation. For example, rather than saying, "You make me feel so stupid when you ask such difficult questions," say, "I feel so stupid when you ask such difficult questions." It's not really their fault if you feel stupid, in the end, is it? The questions they are asking aren't the problem, but rather the problem is *how you feel*. Blaming a colleague like this will only put him/her on the defensive.

The 3 F formula

A very useful formula to deal with uncomfortable situations is the 3 F's. It's a very powerful way to help you be more assertive. We find ourselves using it more and more, and want you to benefit from it as well.

Simply put, it's a way of structuring your message so that you are clear about the situation, take responsibility for your reaction, and offer a solution. Let's look at it step by step.

Step 1:

Facts   Give an objective, factual description of what happened, or what is happening.

Begin this step by saying, "When..." For example: "When you don't offer your opinion in meetings and then send me a long e-mail about it the next day..."

Step 2:

Feelings   This is where you tell the other person how you feel about what happened. People may not always know what you are going through unless you tell them how you feel about it.

Always begin this step by saying, "I feel…" For example: "I feel frustrated because I really need to hear your ideas on the spot rather than a day later."

Step 3:

Future   Now explain what you'd like to happen in the future, your preferred outcome.

Begin this step by saying, "In future, I'd prefer it if you…" or "What I'd like in future is…" For example: "What I'd really like is for you to push yourself to speak up during the meeting, as I really appreciate your thoughts on all our projects."

The 3 F's can go in any order, but we find this is the order that works best. As with anything, you need to practise these steps and keep using them in realistic situations if you are to make them work. It also helps if you write out a script when you are faced with a difficult situation, laying out exactly what you will say, considering any responses you may receive, and your own subsequent replies.

Also, notice that it can really help to add some motivating language to the formula. Don't just tell someone that you'd appreciate a change in their behaviour; tell them why it will be helpful for you both. Emphasise the advantage for both of you in the solution that you are suggesting.

Aha! Moment

The 3 F's can help me in many situations, both professionally and personally.

Using the 3 F's

Imagine you have a client who consistently lets your colleague know of changes to their needs but doesn't inform you, then gets frustrated because you're not up to date. You can use the 3 F's like this:

> *"When you update my colleague on the project without informing me, I feel quite stressed. I'd really appreciate it if you could inform us both at the same time."*

It would be perfectly reasonable to do so. Here's an alternative, more expressive approach:

> *"When you update my colleague on the project without informing me, I feel quite stressed because I can't be as proactive on your behalf as I would like. Perhaps in future you could inform us both at the same time, so that you get the level of service you deserve."*

Adding some language like this will make it much easier for you to be assertive. If you've been avoiding having a conversation because you think it sounds too much like you're complaining (when in fact it's a very reasonable request), making sure that you emphasise the advantage of the new behaviour will help you feel less irritated and more helpful!

Try This

Use the 3 F formula to change these aggressive statements.

1. "When are you going to stop sending me loads of copies of e-mails that I just don't need to see? What a waste of my time, and it just blocks up my inbox. I really don't need it!"

2. "For goodness sake turn that music down. How do you expect me to work with that noise? You're so inconsiderate!"

3. "How many times have I asked you to wash the dishes? I've been working all day and look what I have to face when I get home. You're so selfish, it drives me mad!"

The 3 F's in practice

Here are some more examples of using the 3 F's:

Facts	Feelings	Future
When there are invoices left strewn on my desk...	I feel really disorganised because my desk is a mess and I can't do my job properly.	And what I'd really like is for you to put the invoices in this tray marked 'Invoices' in future.
When I get home and your clothes are strewn all over the house...	I feel really frustrated because I've been working all day and now I have to start working again to tidy up.	What I'd really appreciate is if you'd just put your clothes in the laundry basket next time.

When my calculator is taken from my desk...	I really feel quite irritated because I have to get up and start looking for it.	I don't mind it if you borrow my calculator, but I'd appreciate it if you'd just return it in future.
When you scold me in front of other people...	I feel very embarrassed because it's rather humiliating.	I'd prefer it when you have something to discuss with me, perhaps we can talk in your office?

Try This

The following situations involve a need for assertive behaviour. Role-play each one with a partner. Ask your partner to respond negatively at first, so that you really have to work to find the win-win solution.

1. You are at a restaurant and your steak is tough. Tell the waiter.

2. You are sitting with a friend watching a very interesting movie. Your friend receives a phone call and starts talking loudly, so you are having trouble hearing the television.

⚠️ **Danger Zone**

Beware stating your feelings wrongly. It wouldn't be appropriate to say "I feel you are being inconsiderate..." or "I feel you shouldn't do this." You need to identify your emotion. For example, "I feel disappointed..." or "I feel disturbed...".

Empathy

For a formula like the 3 F's to work, and for you to be able to develop your assertiveness in a dependable way, it's very important to understand the role of empathy in communication. As we discussed at the beginning of this chapter, being assertive involves respecting your own rights and feelings as well as those of others. Being able to put yourself in others' shoes will make this possible for you.

Fast Fact

The most difficult part of the 3 F's seems to be 'Feelings' because many people are uncomfortable saying how they feel. It's important to explain how you are feeling, however, because the other person won't know how you feel unless you tell them. So use words like: frustrated, concerned, disappointed, irritated.

We've noticed in our workshops that a lot of people neglect the second F — the step where you express your feelings. To a colleague who is a bit hot-tempered and consistently raises his voice to people in the office, you might say,

"When you raise your voice at people in the office, I can't get my work done, so I'd appreciate it if you'd stop."

Your hot-tempered colleague might easily think, "It's not my problem if you have concentration issues." But if you make sure to include some indication of how you feel in the formula, it could work better. For example:

"When you raise your voice at people in the office, I feel quite upset and distracted by the negative feeling. I think you can understand that this might be the case for a lot of us. I'd really appreciate it if you could find a way to manage your voice as you deal with your work."

In this second example you are trying to engage the empathy of the hot-tempered colleague to lead to some understanding.

Adding language that shows empathy for them can make such a message even more effective. Take a look at this:

> *"I've noticed that you've been raising your voice a lot in the office lately. I can tell you're feeling a lot of pressure at the moment. That's tough. The thing is, though, when you raise your voice in the office, I feel quite upset and distracted by the negative feeling. I think you can understand that. I'd really appreciate it if you could find a way to manage your voice as you deal with your work. That would be great."*

How does that sound to you? If someone spoke to you that way, would you be more or less likely to respond positively? Consider what it would be like to be on the receiving end of your message, and you will make great progress in crafting successful communication.

Incorporating emotion into our communication

As we have seen, many people find it difficult to express feelings. Some people think it's more important to focus on logic and rationale when they put their points across. But have you ever felt that even though everything makes sense and seems logical, your gut feeling just doesn't feel right? Perhaps the benefits of winning both hearts and minds should really be taken into consideration. If you sometimes feel that your heart isn't convinced by someone's communication, it's important to recognise that you will need to communicate with feeling as well when you have something to say.

Here are some guidelines to help you get in touch with your emotions and begin using them appropriately in your business communication:

1. **Be authentic.** You read about authenticity in Chapter 2.

2. **Ask yourself how you are feeling.** Block out the logical analysis and just focus on how you feel.

3. **Learn to express your feelings simply and honestly.** This will help you communicate, and your relationships will benefit a great deal from expressing more positive feelings. For example, don't hesitate to use language like:

> *"I'm delighted to hear your news."*

> *"I'm really pleased to be working on this project."*

> *"I'm so relieved about that."*

It's important to be clear when your feelings aren't so positive as well. Why? Because if you keep them inside all the time, they can develop into anxiety, resentment, and even depression. As we've said before, being authentic doesn't mean expressing all the emotions you may have in the office. However, it does mean telling your colleagues or clients how you feel when your feelings are affecting your work.

Another important reason to be more aware of your emotions is that this will help to avoid your reactions being perceived as anger and frustration. Both of these responses de-motivate colleagues and upset clients. When we are disappointed, shocked or sad, we often find it most comfortable to respond with anger. Anger is a very blunt instrument, however, and can do so much more harm than good.

Investigating your feelings more carefully can lead to much more productive communication. For example, if a team member comes to you with sloppy work, you might want to say, "What kind of work do you call this? Look at all these mistakes!" But if you recognise that what you really feel is disappointment that your expectations haven't been met, you can use a more assertive approach and say, "I feel disappointed about this. I really need you to check all these things before you bring your work to me," and see how they respond.

If there is discussion in a meeting about a project and you don't agree with the plan, you might be inclined to speak rationally. You might say, "That approach won't work because..." However, if you add some feeling to your communication, you will be using effective 'I' language, and the listener is more likely to be open to your response. Try, "I feel uncomfortable about your approach to this because..." and see what happens.

4. **Encourage other people to express their emotions.**   Ask questions like:

> *"How do you feel about this?"*

> *"What's your gut feeling about this?"*

> *"We've discussed the problem. Now I'd like to know how everyone feels about it."*

> *"What does your instinct tell you?"*

We're not saying that you need to act on your own or your colleagues' gut feelings. We do recommend that these feelings be taken into consideration. Being considerate in your business relationships leads to transparency, to comfort, and to loyalty.

 Fast Fact

Conversations that include both thoughts and feelings are more powerful, more rewarding, and more likely to lead to the right results. They will have a positive effect on all concerned.

Star Tips to enhance your assertiveness

1. Learn to recognise passive, aggressive, passive-aggressive, and assertive behaviour in yourself and others.

2. Promote win-win situations by using assertive behaviour.

3. Communicate what you want in a clear way, respecting your own rights and feelings as well as the rights and feelings of others — this is assertive behaviour.

4. Use other types of behaviour when it is appropriate to do so.

5. Avoid sounding provocative or critical.

6. Practice the 3 F formula to deal with uncomfortable situations. This will help you structure your message assertively.

7. Deliver a clean, clear statement of your point of view by using 'I' language.

8. Investigate your feelings so that your reactions are not perceived as anger.

9. Be sure to express your most important feelings appropriately, so that you don't become anxious or depressed.

10. Encourage others to express their feelings as well, so that you understand what's going on with your colleagues and clients.

TELEPHONE SKILLS

7

"*I have always wished for a computer that would be as easy to use as my telephone. My wish came true. I no longer know how to use my telephone.*"

Bjarne Stronstrup

The telephone is undoubtedly the most important tool in the field of communications, especially when you consider that time is at a premium, and instant decisions can often make a big difference. Even with the speed of e-mail, the telephone must still come out on top purely because you can hear a real voice and form an instant relationship. Also, when you send an e-mail, you don't know how much time will pass before it is read.

However, a telephone conversation is not face-to-face, so there are no visual cues or non-verbal cues from body language, which help us to better understand and connect with others when listening and speaking. In this chapter we share with you some suggestions for making the most of all your telephone interactions, to ensure that people will enjoy calling you and receiving your calls.

Why use the telephone?

Telephones have been around since 1877, and are most certainly an essential piece of equipment. Just think of all the things we can do on the telephone.

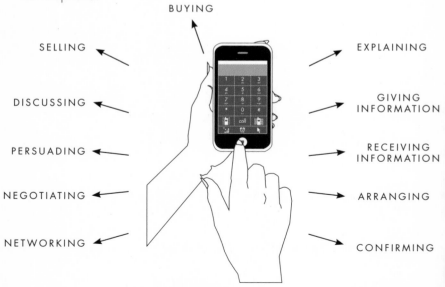

BUYING

SELLING

DISCUSSING

PERSUADING

NEGOTIATING

NETWORKING

EXPLAINING

GIVING INFORMATION

RECEIVING INFORMATION

ARRANGING

CONFIRMING

If these are not already reason enough to use the telephone, here are three more great ones.

1. **Speed.** It's so much quicker to pick up a telephone and dial a number than it is to write a letter or an e-mail. We even have last number redial and speed dial to save us the trouble of dialling the entire telephone number.

2. **Personal contact.** Unlike e-mail, the telephone gives you a chance to hear the other person's voice. Although you cannot see them, you can build up a mental picture of them and form a relationship with them. You can learn a lot about a person through voice contact on the telephone.

3. **Instant feedback.** Unlike written communication, on the telephone you can receive an immediate response or an answer to a question, or discuss a topic in more detail.

 Aha! Moment

Even if I'm an e-mail addict, I must use the telephone to build relationships and create bonds.

How to upset people on the telephone

There are many ways you can annoy the other person on the telephone! Here are our suggestions.

1. **Sound abrupt, especially when you pick up the call.** The caller has interrupted your work, and they should know they've disturbed you.

2. **Speak in a really formal and stilted manner.** This will turn people off and they will want to hang up quickly.

3. **Don't include any pauses.**   Just speak continuously without coming up for air. This way there will be no awkward gaps, no time for you to think, and no time for the other person to think.

4. **Speak at the same time as eating or chewing the end of your pen.** That way your speech will be unclear and muffled, and the caller will soon get the message that you don't want to talk.

5. **Tap away on your computer while speaking.**   This will put the other person off.

Fast Fact

Of course we are having a joke with you here, and these are not things that you should do on the telephone if you want to gain a reputation as a thoughtful communicator. What you *should* do instead is:

- Make a commitment to the caller by giving them your full attention.

- Speak in a friendly, informal tone, to help you build relationships.

- Remember that people need time to think on the telephone too, so don't feel obliged to fill every gap.

- Don't talk and type!

How would you rate your telephone skills?

Here are some questions to check on your telephone etiquette. Answer the questions truthfully. If lots of your answers are in the 'sometimes' or 'rarely' column, you need to consider how you can improve your telephone skills.

	Always	Sometimes	Rarely
I answer the telephone on or before the third ring.			
When I leave my desk I tell someone where I'm going and when I'll be back.			
I identify my name and department at the beginning of incoming and outgoing calls.			

	Always	Sometimes	Rarely
I consciously try to project a positive impression.			
I speak clearly and directly into the mouthpiece.			
I give undivided attention to each caller.			
I apologise when callers have been inconvenienced.			
I ask callers first before putting them on hold or transferring them.			
I avoid using "Um", "Er" and other waffle words.			
I try not to put callers on hold for more than 30 seconds.			
I make proper notes before making any call.			
I don't consider callers to be an interruption of my work.			
I am patient and attentive on the telephone.			
I smile while I'm on the telephone.			
I convey energy, interest and enthusiasm in my tone of voice.			
I try to make sure every caller is a satisfied caller.			
I try to create a bond and a partnership with all callers.			

Touch up your telephone manner

We cannot over-emphasise how important it is to develop a great telephone manner. Without the benefit of being able to see a person's body language or facial expressions, it's essential to put some enthusiasm into your voice on the telephone. Compare these two openings:

#1   Hello.

I'm looking for Richard Tan, please.

Yes, speaking.

Oh, hi Richard, this is Susan Wood from Pioneer Construction.

OK, how can I help you?

#2   Hello, Richard Tan here.

Hello Richard, I'm Susan Wood from Pioneer Construction.

Hi Susan, good to hear from you.

Can you see the difference? The second opening creates a bond, shows some feelings, and starts to develop a real relationship. And it does so in fewer sentences than the first one!

 Aha! Moment

I will never get a second chance to create a great first impression!

"Hello" and other weak telephone language

One of the biggest irritations with the telephone has to be when someone answers the phone with just "Hello." It will almost inevitably lead to the caller saying, "Is that...?" Another thing that really annoys others is when, for example, you answer the phone with "Hello, this is Shirley", and then the caller says "Hello, can I speak to Shirley please?"

When you answer your phone, remember to put some enthusiasm into your voice and show an interest in the caller. Use friendly expressions like:

"How nice to hear from you."

"It's nice to hear your voice for a change."

"This is a nice surprise. Thank you."

Expressions like these start off the conversation on the right note. Remember also that on the telephone you need to use your voice well, with variance in pitch and intonation. All these things will have an effect on the way the other person receives your message.

Here are some other weak expressions we suggest you avoid on the telephone.

Instead of	Say
Hello.	Good morning, Mr Tay's office. Maggie speaking.
I'll call you back soon.	I'll call you back within the next 30 minutes.
You've got the wrong department.	I'm sorry, you've been put through to Sales. You need Purchasing. I'll transfer you.

What do you want me to do about it?	How can I help you, Mrs Lim?
No problem.	You're welcome. My pleasure.
That's impossible.	I'll do my best to help you with this.
Who is this?	May I have your name please? Who's calling please?
I don't know.	I'm not sure, but I'll try to find out for you.
The only thing I can do is...	The best thing I can do is...
Sorry to keep you waiting.	Thank you for holding.

Something else to remember is a smile. I know it may sound corny to smile when no one can see you, but a smile really does make a difference. The person at the other end will be able to hear it and pick up on your good mood.

 Try This

Say this sentence without smiling:

"This is Martha from Sales. How can I help you?"

Now say it again with a real smile on your face.

I guarantee you even put some intonation into your voice the second time around. And didn't you feel better too?

Fast Fact

It's difficult to feel gloomy when you have a smile on your face, so when you smile your spirits will automatically rise. This is bound to be noticed by the other person, even on the telephone.

Take pride in your telephone professionalism

If you are to establish a real bond and partnership with all the customers, colleagues and clients that you deal with in the course of your work, you need to project a professional image on the telephone. Here is our advice on how you can take pride in your telephone skills:

Pitch — There's nothing worse than listening to someone talk in a high pitch. Speaking in a lower voice tone is thought to help you have more control of a telephone conversation. Also, try to project your voice rather than to shout. There is a difference. Speaking more directly into the mouthpiece will help.

Rate — Slow down your speech on the telephone. This will give the caller a chance to take in what you have to say.

Inflection — Use correct tone for emphasis, with a rise and fall in your voice.

Diction — Don't mumble or slur your words. Make an effort to pronounce each word carefully.

Energy — A lot of your energy is lost over the telephone lines. This means you need even more energy on the phone than you would have face to face. So inject some more zip into your voice on the phone!

Fast Fact

Customers are not an interruption of your job. Customers are your job! You must create a positive impression in every call!

Techniques to remember when using the telephone

When making calls, it works best to:

1. **Plan your calls.** Make a note beforehand of what you want to say and what you hope to achieve by the call. Note down the key questions you want to ask. Having all relevant information in front of you when you make the call will also help you to speak more confidently.

2. **Breathe!** Sounds easy enough, yes? But many of us are shallow breathers, so this makes us sound tired on the phone. When the phone is ringing at the other end, take a big breath in and exhale, then when you answer you'll not only feel better but the caller will hear more energy in your voice.

3. **Identify yourself.** Introduce yourself clearly and state the reason for your call. Be as clear and concise as possible, and remember to smile.

4. **Ask the recipient if it's a convenient time.** This is especially important if your call may take a while.

5. **Listen attentively.** This means putting everything down except your plan, a pen and some paper to make notes. It just won't work if you are drinking your coffee, replying to an e-mail and checking your

horoscope in the daily paper. Multitasking, this is not! Take notes on what the other party is saying too, so you can remember the key points of the conversation and the action items.

6. **Visualise the person.** Even if you don't know the other person, imagine where they are sitting and think about them, just as a reminder that you are engaged in a two-way conversation.

7. **Summarise any important points.** At the end of the call, use phrases like, "Let me just summarise the key points now," or "As I understand it ..."

8. **Thank the caller at the end of the call.** For example, "Thanks for your time, Nicole," or "I'll be in touch again soon."

When receiving calls, it's best to:

1. **Breathe (again!).** When the phone starts ringing, take a very big breath and then answer the phone. You will continue speaking on the exhale of that breath and the caller will hear energy in your voice!

2. **Use an appropriate greeting.** We've all heard this many times before, but still it needs saying again. "Yes", or "Hello" just won't work. Identify yourself clearly. Try not to make this too long. There's nothing more annoying than someone saying very quickly and almost incoherently, "*GoodmorningAbbottConstructionthisisMrTan'sofficeMaryspeaking Howmaylhelpyou?*"

3. **Listen attentively.** Visualise the caller, and summarise — as in the previous section.

4. **Thank the caller at the end of the call.** For example, "Thanks for your call," or "Lovely to speak to you, John."

Fast Fact

People like to hear their names, and it enhances the feeling of friendliness. Use the other person's name wherever appropriate during a telephone call.

Myth Buster

If I am cut off during a telephone conversation, I should just wait for the other person to call me back.

The etiquette here is that the person who instigated the call should be the one who calls back. If that's not you, just sit tight. But if it is, get dialling!

Voicemail

While we have to agree that voicemail is a great thing, and it has an important role to play, it is no substitute for a live human voice. Very often these days, people activate their voicemail just to screen their calls. What a waste of everyone's time!

Remember, time is usually of the essence, so if people can't get hold of you they may go somewhere else. If you must activate your voicemail, do update your message frequently so that it gives callers an idea of when you are likely to return their call. And then please do so!

Danger Zone

Beware of leaving stilted, overly formal voice messages that can sound unfriendly and unwelcoming. Speak slowly and with good intonation, making your message sound friendly, and taking care to repeat important numbers.

When is it better not to call?

Here are some occasions when it is better not to use the telephone:

1. When you have to give bad news. This is better given in person.

2. When a formal record is needed. An e-mail or letter would be best at these times.

3. When you have to convey complex information. This is better put in writing.

4. When you have a difficult situation to discuss. It would be better to do so face-to-face so you can see the other person's reactions and adapt accordingly.

5. When you need to contact very busy, senior people. Perhaps an e-mail would be best in this case.

6. When the recipient will need time to consider their response. E-mail may be best here. (To learn more about effective e-mail, read Shirley's book, *E-mail Etiquette*, also part of the Success Skills series.)

Star Tips for better telephone communication

1. Put lots of enthusiasm into your voice on the phone. A lot of energy is lost over the telephone lines.

2. Use the telephone to develop relationships, increase understanding and create bonds.

3. Be friendly and natural on the phone, using informal language as much as possible.

4. Vary your pitch and tone so that the conversation remains engaging.

5. Show an interest in the other person by using their name and friendly expressions.

6. Avoid weak, unhelpful expressions. They can be very frustrating and leave a bad impression.

7. Aim to create a positive impression in every telephone conversation.

8. Give your full attention to every caller. That means don't talk and type!

9. Give people time to think. You don't need to fill every gap.

10. Take stock of your telephone manner frequently, and make appropriate adjustments.

COMMUNICATING IN TEAMS

*"Coming together is a
beginning; keeping together
is progress; working together
is success."*

Henry Ford

8

If you have started using the techniques we have discussed so far, such as listening more actively, developing your consistency and credibility, thinking through your message and expressing it clearly, asserting yourself appropriately and respecting others, it's very likely that you are already feeling the teambuilding effects of better communication. If you can continue to lead by example, the people you work with may be picking up some of your new techniques as well (although don't be surprised if some of them don't even notice!)

Everyone's on the team

In reality, all communication at work is teamwork. Even if you are just bringing someone from another department up to date on your own department's activities, you're acting as a member of the team. A lot has been said and written about the importance of transparency in business so that both investors and clients can trust the organisations with which they are involved. Transparency *within* the organisation is equally important.

'Silo' mentality

Many organisations suffer from what's known as 'silo' behaviour. Each department functions as a singular unit, keeping all their business and information in their own storage silo or tower, protecting their territory, rebuffing outsiders. When the ones seen as 'outsiders' are in fact insiders, the company as a whole — as well as the individuals involved — can only suffer.

This sort of thing regularly happens between sales and accounts departments, accounts and creative departments, front and back offices, and any number of other departments that differ in philosophy and therefore in approach. Managing this problem and improving the situation takes time and effort, and above all takes communication. Everyone involved must be persuaded that supporting each other's efforts is, by its nature, a win-win situation.

Fast Fact

Teams comprise many different personalities. Getting them to work together effectively is not easy, but it is essential to organisational health and prosperity.

The 3 C's of effective teamwork

When lots of people come together, effective **communication** is one thing, but it can so easily go wrong if there is no **co-operation**. Once everyone starts working together towards common goals that are understood and appreciated by all, there can be **collaboration**. Collaboration means a true group effort.

Naturally it's best if such a collaborative approach can be incorporated into the entire organisation's culture, and this requires that people at all levels agree. It doesn't mean, however, that individuals can't make a significant difference by improving their day-to-day communication and leading by example. Absolutely they can!

 Danger Zone

Watch out for thinking that your work will be easier if you keep what you're doing to yourself. People will help you if you are willing to help them.

Collaborative teamwork is helped along by a number of things, including:

- **Willingness on the part of each team member.** People who don't want to be involved are obstacles to progress.

- **A working environment that allows the team the freedom to develop ideas and plans without unreasonable limitations.** Teams need time, space and resources.

- **Clear responsibilities for, and expectations of, the team and its members.** Confusion leads to resentment.

Fast Fact

Remember, the 3 C's of effective teamwork are:

Communication

+

Co-operation

=

Collaboration

Communicating from the start

The common denominator for all of these requirements is, of course, communication. It's not enough to sign on and get to work. Each team member must understand the reason the team has been put together and the role they are expected to play in it. This must be communicated to them, and things will progress most smoothly if they each express their understanding of the situation once it has been laid out.

It's not helpful to have meetings where people are wondering what they're doing there in the first place! Start using the technique of paraphrasing, and encourage others to do so, right from the very beginning of the team effort ("So what you're saying I need to do is...", "Do you mean that...", "Let me make sure I understand the process...", etc). This will help avoid misunderstandings and develop a common goal.

The rules of the game

If we asked you to come up with a list of what type of communication you believe works best for teams, you would probably mention characteristics like openness, clarity, and mutual respect, among others. Well, why not have this type of communication be the rule, rather than merely an ideal? Developing guidelines for communication in your team will lead to more effective meetings because people will be encouraged to behave to a common standard, agreed by the group. These guidelines can be as broad or as specific as you see fit, although we believe it really pays to be concrete so that they aren't open to highly different interpretations, which could lead to more confusion rather than less. Let's look at some examples here.

For team meetings you might want to suggest the following:

- Have a clear agenda, communicated to the team before the meeting.

- Be on time.

- Silence mobile phones and only use laptops for meeting purposes, not to work while others are talking.

- Listen actively and respectfully, avoiding interruptions.

- Speak clearly, in a structured manner (unless brainstorming, when stream-of-consciousness can work just fine).

- Appoint someone (different each time) to give a summary of each meeting and its outcome at the end, for a common take-away.

For written communication, guidelines like these can be helpful:

- Structure e-mails for maximum clarity (for very helpful tips on how to do this, see Shirley's book in the Success Skills series, *E-mail Etiquette*).

- Copy all team members on all team-related e-mails. This will keep activities transparent and avoid confusion, and you will not have to repeat yourself.

- Don't always use e-mail. Maintain the flow of communication by speaking face to face as often as possible!

Help yourself by helping others

Beyond developing guidelines for meetings and e-mails, you may also encourage an overall guideline for behaviour, one that is the hallmark of high-performing teams (as opposed to mere work units). This is one that says that in order for the team to succeed, *everyone involved must have the success of everyone else at heart.*

We so often forget that we can help meet our own objectives by helping our teammates meet theirs. People worry that if they help others, they will be overwhelmed by the amount of work this generates, so that even within small teams you have silos developing. What open, helpful behaviour often generates, however, is an abundance of good feeling within the team, of greater willingness, and a reduction in stress levels. If each team member endeavours to make the rest of the team look good, then the team will absolutely look good. Encourage this attitude in the group. Notice how much happier people are to come to meetings and to participate positively and respectfully. Also notice how the quality not only of the teamwork but also of the output improves.

Positive thinking and productivity

Silo behaviour is protective behaviour, and protective behaviour is by its nature negative. When people are protective, they are assuming that collaborating would be threatening in some way. Information stops flowing. But information is power, and an organisation without a flow of information is a weak one.

 Fast Fact

Our brains function more creatively when we are thinking positively. 'No' is the least creative word in any language.

In order for work to flow smoothly, then, people must have a positive view of the benefits of engaging with each other, as well as a positive view of the situations they find themselves in. This doesn't mean that you all have to like each other, and it doesn't mean that you have to pretend that a crisis isn't happening. What it does mean is that you stay positive about your involvement and your ability to make something of it. You can't manage what you don't accept, and rejecting a situation is very uncreative. Morale suffers. Business stagnates.

Try This

This is an improvisation game called 'That's Great'. In it, each group of four people gets one chair, and the person in the chair is the CEO, who decides on the type of company it is. The remaining three players are employees of this company, and have to come up with ideas for the worst things they can imagine could happen to that type of company. So for example if the CEO says they are a noodle company, one of the other players can say, "Boss! Boss! It's terrible! The government has just outlawed anything that's long and thin!"

No matter what the boss feels at this point, he/she must begin by saying "That's great!" and must proceed to explain why this is a wonderful thing for the company. The boss might respond with, "That's great! We know that parents will spend almost any amount on their kids these days. This will push us into noodles shaped like animals and sports cars for the kiddy market. Fantastic!" Then the CEO fields the second problem, and the third, after which one of the other players takes the seat, becomes CEO, decides what type of company they run, and off they go again.

Again, the point of such an exercise is not to tell you to imagine that all apparently bad things are good, but rather to encourage you to consider how problems may be opportunities. Playing this game will show you just how easy it is to react negatively to a situation without really considering it from all sides. As you play it, listen to the voice in your head. Maybe it is telling you, "This is impossible! I can't use this problem!" If this happens, try to override the voice with the enthusiasm of your "That's great!" and you will see how this frees you to be more creative. This in turn will help you have more confidence in your ideas.

Aha! Moment

My brain can grapple with any problem if I can just stop worrying and get out of its way.

The positive role of negative thinking

In most groups there are people who take a negative stance. They can be extremely hard to work with, as it feels like they are highly critical, or that they constantly need to limit the ideas of others. While we encourage everyone to develop their positive thinking in order to use more of their brains and be more solution-oriented, we also want to make sure that negative thinking gets a bit of respect.

It's all about timing. Positive thinking has its place, and is supremely helpful in communication. Negative thinking also has its place, and critics play an important role in any process. The key is to make sure that positive thinking and negative thinking are used at the right time. Groups can avoid the limiting, often upsetting effect of negative thinkers simply by making sure that they understand the appropriate time and place for their comments. Criticism in itself is not bad. It is feedback. It is important. Ideas must be criticised in order to test their strength. However, just as with most other forms of communication, criticism must be voiced at the right time to be useful.

Teams can choose when this time is. By setting guidelines that prohibit interruption when someone is speaking during a meeting, you will avoid a lot of the negative effects of criticism. We largely interrupt when we don't agree. Think about your meetings. Don't most interruptions begin with the word 'But'? Give people the chance to get to the end of their idea or their message.

Guidelines for responding to ideas can also be encouraged, for example by indicating the value of highlighting what is useful in the idea offered before pointing out its weaknesses.

 Myth Buster

We waste time by listening to ideas that have no value.

Value is subjective. Be careful not to judge an idea too soon, because someone else on the team may be able to see the importance of it in a way that isn't immediately obvious to you.

Another very effective technique that teams can use is to delay criticism until as many thoughts have been put out on the table as possible. People are more likely to feel safe and supported when offering their ideas if that is the only type of communication that is allowed. This is particularly true at the brainstorming stage of any team effort. If critics jump in too fast, others will be less willing to offer ideas, and both morale and productivity will suffer.

Try This

During a brainstorming meeting, assign a certain amount of time exclusively for the offering of ideas. Make sure everything gets written down on a flipchart, or on flipchart paper on the table, so that nothing gets lost. Don't allow any criticism of ideas during the brainstorming time, insisting that everyone imagine that there are no limits on what can happen. Forget about budgets or time constraints, since thinking about these will reduce creativity, as well as fun! Allow ideas to flow and to grow.

Once everyone has been able to participate freely, and only then, start taking a critical look at what's on the paper, so that you can choose the strongest and most practical ideas from the collection. But don't throw away the others! They might be useful at another time.

Respecting the power of positive thinking, as well as the importance of more critical thought, will boost morale and help to bind the team together. Agreeing on guidelines that facilitate various ways of thinking, at the right time and place, and sticking to these guidelines, will turn the pain of meetings into pleasure.

Star Tips for improving team communication

1. Strive for an open flow of communication in the organisation. 'Silo' behaviour is very dangerous.

2. Start out the way you want to continue — by making sure the whole team has a very clear understanding of the common goals.

3. Ensure effective guidelines are set down for team behaviour, both spoken and written. This is invaluable in maintaining cohesion.

4. Encourage positive thinking in the team. Many people react negatively to problems. Positive thinking will lead to higher morale and more creative solutions.

5. Remember that critical or negative thinkers have an important role to play in teams. The key is to make sure they play this role at the right time.

6. Encourage freedom to develop ideas by ensuring the environment is conducive to creative thought.

7. Help others and you will be helping yourself. Teamwork is not easy, but it is essential for the success of every organisation.

8. Make sure all team members feel appreciated and that their opinions are valued.

9. Encourage regular team talks to provide feedback and motivation.

10. Deal with conflict between team members immediately and positively. (Chapter 10 will tell you more about coping with conflict.)

COMMUNICATING ACROSS CULTURES

9

"To effectively communicate, we must realise that we are all different in the way we perceive the world, and use this understanding as a guide to our communication with others."

Anthony Robbins

Anthony Robbins couldn't have said it more clearly. What we say to one person may mean something quite different to another, because of their background, their culture, or even their mood, and the sooner we realise this, the quicker we will be able to adapt to the communication needs of the people we need to and want to talk to.

What is culture?

Culture is a shared system of beliefs, attitudes, values, expectations and norms of behaviour. Members of a culture often have similar beliefs and theories on how people should behave, think and communicate, and they tend to act on those beliefs in much the same way.

From group to group, cultures differ considerably. When you communicate with someone from a different culture, you normally do so using the theories and beliefs of your own culture. However, when your audience receives your message, they do so based on the assumptions of their own culture. As a result of basic cultural differences, misunderstandings can easily occur, and often do.

If you are to communicate effectively across cultures, it's important not to judge other people by your own standards. It is essential to retain an open mind, and remember that your own cultural background is not necessarily superior to anyone else's.

 Danger Zone

Many people mistakenly assume that other people's attitudes and lives are like their own. Our aim should not be to try to treat people in the way we wish to be treated, but rather treat them in the way *they* want to be treated.

Ethnocentrism

Ethnocentrism is the belief that one's own cultural background is superior to all others. This creates a barrier to effective communication because the mind remains closed to new information and the heart to new feelings.

Ethnocentric people tend to form pre-conceived judgements of different cultures based on one experience, or based on limited evidence. They tend to be quite critical when they are outside their own country, no matter where they go, because they are constantly comparing where they are to what they are used to. Naturally, this hinders their ability to experience the new place, and the new people, openly and fully. Beyond this, their attitude is offensive to the citizens of their host country, and inhibits the development of meaningful relationships. Remember in the chapter on listening, where we talked about listening to understand rather than to agree? We make the same recommendation here, with regard to other cultures.

Aha! Moment

If I am open to other cultures, I will learn to understand them better. I don't necessarily have to agree with them or behave like them. It just helps to increase my knowledge.

Stereotyping

You don't have to be ethnocentric to be prone to stereotyping. Many people may have formed an opinion of people from other cultures, based not on direct experience but rather on images in the media and stories of friends or colleagues.

Alison has felt this quite often during her life abroad:

> It's hard to find anyone in the world who doesn't have
> an idea of what a 'typical American' is like. This comes
> both from how often America's political and international
> activities are in the news, as well as from the widespread
> reach of Hollywood and other American products. I often
> get asked where I come from, and I usually ask people to
> guess. Nine times out of ten, they guess wrongly. When
> they are wrong, I ask them to guess again, and usually
> they are wrong again. I can only imagine this is because
> I am not overweight, I'm not running along a beach in a
> sexy bathing suit (at least not when I'm in the back of a
> taxi, standing in a queue, or conducting a workshop), I
> am not loud (at least not the first time you meet me), and
> I don't carry a gun. But millions of Americans look and
> act a lot like I do.

Take a moment now to consider your impressions of people from cultures you have yet to experience yourself. What comes to mind first about them?

French

_____

_____

_____

Japanese

_____

_____

_____

Russian

_____

_____

_____

Nigerian

_____

_____

_____

Mexican

_____

_____

_____

Some of these stereotypes may well be positive, indicating talent, or good nature. But even so, any stereotype will affect how you react to someone from that culture when you actually meet them. If you meet a Latin American who isn't a good dancer, and you say, "Hey, that's weird, I thought all Latinos had rhythm," you aren't looking at the person as an individual, and they are likely to feel less warmly toward you as a result.

Think about yourself. Do you represent the common stereotype of your own culture? No doubt you have many of your own, special, very independent characteristics. That's all the proof you need.

Aha! Moment

When I take the time to investigate a culture, I will begin to find how many variations there are within it.

I know what I heard, but I'm not sure what you said

The effectiveness of any communication will depend on the type of language you use and the particular words you choose. Some words may have different meanings to different people, even if they are both native speakers of the same language. Many things, for example our experience and our culture, will affect our understanding. Alison has a story to share about this.

> I was fixing a date with a boyfriend once (well, it's happened many times in my life, but I'm just going to tell you about this once!). He was American, like me. We were talking on the phone. When we had agreed on a date and time, he said, "I'll pencil it in now. I'm sorry I have to do this, but I have trouble remembering my schedule." Immediately I began to feel a bit hurt. Why was he only pencilling me in? Was the date fixed or not? If it were fixed, shouldn't he be writing it in pen? To me, pencilling something in means keeping your options open. Also, when he said that he had trouble remembering his schedule, I took it to mean that he wasn't sure if he was free or not.
>
> Knowing that it's dangerous both to jump to conclusions and to keep these things inside, I gently asked the question, "So are we meeting or not?"

"Of course we are," he said. "I've just pencilled it in!"

"But you've put it in pencil," I replied.

There was a short silence. Then he said, "Oh! I see what you mean. In fact, I'm not using pencil at all. I'm typing it into my computer."

If I hadn't clarified what his words meant to him, rather than to me, I might have let the hurt build up and become resentment. Having checked with him, however, I learned about how he used the expression "to pencil something in", and we avoided this misunderstanding in the future.

 Fast Fact

We can't assume that we know what the other person means. It's always best always to ask questions to clarify.

Beyond checking with the other person on what they mean, and what they think you meant, what else can you do to help?

Prejudgement is often proved wrong

Whether or not we are aware of it, or willing to admit it, we often form preconceptions about people and about issues, and these can affect the success of our communication. For example, some people attend Shirley's writing workshop expecting it to be very boring, because they simply can't imagine a writing workshop being any other way. This is a common prejudgement, and one that is proved wrong just moments into the workshop because it's a fun learning experience from start to finish.

Just as you might avoid a writing workshop for fear that it will be boring, and miss out on a great experience, you might avoid someone from a different culture because of a prejudgement based on hearsay, and miss out on a great business opportunity, or learning experience, or friendship.

It's completely natural to prejudge both people and events, as we are guided by our past experiences. However, it's very important to stay open to the possibility of things being different to how you imagine them. You might miss a fantastic career, education, or personal opportunity because you had decided something really good was going to be bad. Listen to what you're saying to yourself about someone you've just met or a meeting you have to attend, and ask yourself if you may have made a judgement too early in the game.

 Try This

When you are dreading going to an event or a meeting, take moment to remember all the previous occasions when you've been pleasantly surprised after similar feelings. This will remind you that it's only by being open to change that you will have a true opportunity to make the most of the present.

Understanding where people are coming from

The way we were raised, our belief systems, our religion, our education, our culture — all these things will have an effect on the way we communicate, and on the way we receive communication from others. This is of course very obvious when people from two different nationalities communicate, but it is still the case for people from more similar cultures. For example, Shirley is from the UK and Alison is from the US but has a British mother. Both of us are women. Both of us were brought up speaking English. Both of us come from a family of four. We are nonetheless constantly asking each other what an expression or a word means when the other one is talking. It is by no means a chore. On the contrary, it's really good fun, and continually adds cement to our relationship.

There is an unfortunate arrogance in not taking time to try and understand where other people are, literally, coming from. Communication is much smoother, and therefore much more satisfying, when we learn about others and adapt to them. This effort often leads to greater trust and respect, and an effort on the part of others to understand us as well.

Fast Fact

Intercultural communication doesn't just refer to people from different countries. An American engineer might have trouble understanding the concepts of an American ballet dancer just as much as a Chinese engineer might have trouble understanding a British engineer, even if they are both speaking English.

The same principle applies when people from the same culture talk together as when people from different cultures do. And that is, you can only be sure you are being understood if you have been curious enough about the other party to know what type of language they will understand.

I know what I said, but I'm not sure what you heard

Communication with people of our own culture in our own country is difficult enough. Intercultural communication provides even more challenges. Imagine, then, relocating to a completely new country. Shirley has a story to share on this:

I lived in Sheffield in the UK all my life until I got my first teaching post in Singapore. Fresh from teacher-training college, and never having been overseas before, I landed in Singapore in August 1983 and was met by my boss and her colleague. I sat in the back of the car talking all the way, in the only accent I knew, which was my northern England (Yorkshire) accent: "Oh it's so clean 'ere ... look at all't trees, and all't boats out there on't water ... gosh I've never been on a plane so long in me life ... it's so 'ot 'ere intit? ... thank goodness for air conditionin'." (It's very difficult to write this in my colloquial Yorkshire accent, but hopefully you will get the gist there!)

I thought it was strange that neither of the two ladies in the front said a word. I found out much later that as soon as they dropped me off at my new home, they telephoned the lady in London who had interviewed me for the job, and told her, "We don't understand a word Shirley says. Her accent is too hard to understand. We are going to send her back on the first plane tomorrow." The British lady in London laughed and said, "Oh please give her a chance. I'm sure she'll soon realise that she has to adapt her accent. I'm sure she'll settle down and you'll start communicating better pretty soon."

All I can say is, thank goodness for that lovely lady in the UK. I quickly realised that my Yorkshire accent was very difficult for people to understand, and as I was the newcomer in a different country, I couldn't expect everyone else to change. So I had to start speaking more slowly, and pronouncing my words more carefully, really enunciating the beginnings and the endings. Fortunately I was a quick learner, and not only did I learn how I needed to communicate to be understood in Singapore, my boss, colleagues, and students also learned a little more about Yorkshire culture. Talk about sink or swim!

When I go back to the UK, it's amazing how quickly I revert to my real Yorkshire accent. However, as soon as I get to Singapore again, I automatically adjust. As they say, "When in Rome …"!

 Danger Zone

Don't always think that first impressions are the right impressions. Sometimes it takes a while, especially in new cultures, to adapt, to change, to settle in.

Shirley's experience on that first trip to Singapore could have been very different. Her boss could have sent her home because of difficulties she thought Shirley would have adjusting to a new culture. Shirley could have left for the same reason. Adjusting to different cultures takes time, and involves many more experiences — being willing to try new foods, visiting new places, meeting people from many ethnic backgrounds, experiencing new things, doing lots of things completely out of your comfort zones. Adapting and adjusting can be a huge challenge, but it's one that can open up your mind and your heart to brand new worlds, new friends, new possibilities, and in many cases a new life.

The world is in your office

Many businesses today operate on a global scale, and our culturally diverse workforce is made up of people from different countries, ethnic backgrounds, races, religion and family structures. If we are to communicate effectively with all these different people, it is important to keep an open mind and try to learn as much as possible about their various cultures, and be sensitive to them. You can have a lot of fun in doing so, and can make lots of new friends too.

Star Tips for communicating across cultures

1. Avoid assumptions, acknowledging and accepting that there are distinctions between your own culture and other people's.

2. Prejudgement closes off avenues for communication. Stay open to the ways of others, seeking the common ground that will lead to understanding.

3. Show respect. Learn how respect is communicated in different cultures (gestures, eye contact, symbols, signs, etc).

4. Accept that you may have to change your habits or mindset when communicating across cultures.

5. Be patient. Sometimes persistence will be necessary when communicating with someone from a different culture.

6. Send clear messages. Make sure all your written, verbal and non-verbal communication is clear, reliable and consistent.

7. Avoid treating one person as a stereotype of a particular group, but see them instead as a unique human being with individual qualities and attributes.

8. Treat people in the way they wish to be treated, not necessarily as you wish to be treated.

9. Take time to investigate different cultures and you will find many variations within each.

10. Never assume you know what another person means. It's always best to clarify.

COPING WITH CONFLICT

"Absence of communication between necessarily linked parties ensures eventual conflict."

Eric Parslow

Communication is all about understanding and bringing people together, but there's no guarantee that they will always agree. With so many different people and personalities in our workplace, it's not surprising that a degree of conflict occurs. We've all experienced situations where different people with different needs and goals have come into conflict.

Conflict is very damaging

If conflict is not handled positively and constructively, the results can be very damaging. A minor dispute can easily turn into a major argument or confrontation. A disagreement can quickly turn into personal animosity. Teamwork breaks down, and a downward spiral of negativity and blame will be the result.

The previous chapters in this book have given you all the tools you need to help you deal with conflict — listening actively, speaking effectively, using appropriate tone, being assertive, and appreciating differences. However, sometimes no matter what you try, there will still be problems.

We all know people who 'rub us up the wrong way' or whose mannerisms irritate us. Unfortunately, many people let off their steam to friends, colleagues or partners, instead of dealing with the friction head on. This very often makes matters worse because the friction builds up inside you. One of the best things you can do is to sit down and talk, preferably before the situation gets out of hand.

 Fast Fact

Effective communication skills can go a long way towards resolving friction. Weak communication skills leave you in a boat without a paddle.

Watch for signs of conflict

As you will have read in the chapter on teamwork, a certain amount of friction is inevitable where more than one person is working on the same project and guidelines for behaviour aren't in place or aren't being respected. It's good to be on the watch for signs that suggest a breakdown in communication or in understanding, or a difference that will interfere with the team's ability to work well together. Learn to recognise these signs before they turn into an all-out war. Here are some of them:

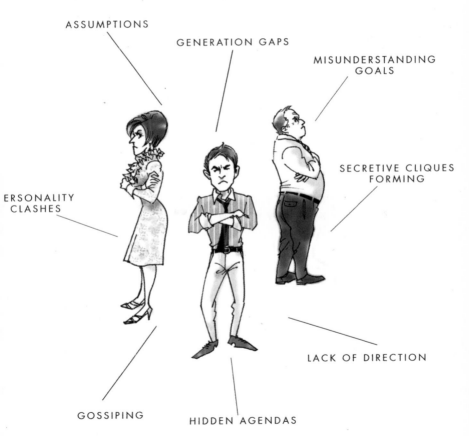

ASSUMPTIONS

GENERATION GAPS

MISUNDERSTANDING GOALS

SECRETIVE CLIQUES FORMING

ERSONALITY CLASHES

LACK OF DIRECTION

GOSSIPING

HIDDEN AGENDAS

Fast Fact

Investigating and resolving conflict as soon as you feel it can act as a glue that strengthens the team.

Seven deadly sins of dealing with conflict

Being aware of what not to do in conflict situations will certainly help you to figure out the best course of action. If you want to make matters worse, then here are some behaviours to practice next time you encounter conflict. These behaviours will never resolve tension; they will merely intensify it.

1. **Shouting.** Not many people respond well when you raise your voice. Shouting will often produce shouting in return. It is even worse in a public setting when other people are witness to your slanging match.

2. **Sarcasm.** Very often disguised as snide humour, sarcastic comments and subtle digs will only amplify the tension and friction that already exist.

3. **Blaming.** Using a critical, finger-pointing, fault-finding approach turns everything quite personal. Emphasising what is wrong will also take away the focus from the issue that needs resolving.

4. **Defensiveness.** When you react defensively, it very often involves you interrupting, and raising your voice. You're not listening. Reacting in this way is a sure way to put walls between you and the other party.

5. **Insults.**   Name-calling and personal abuse will only make matters more unbearable. If you use this approach, people will not even want to work with you at all, let alone resolve the situation.

6. **Threats.** Ultimatums generally backfire. "Do it this way or else" might get something done in the short term, but can create lasting resentment and defiance.

7. **Complaining.**   Some people don't want to approach the source directly, but prefer to tell everyone else about it. If you complain constantly about friction, people will just turn away from you and no one will want to listen to you. Complaining and backstabbing can also stimulate gossip and rumours.

 Aha! Moment

If I want to resolve tension, I must not resort to name-calling, sarcasm or any other negative behaviours, no matter how tempted I may be.

Seven secrets of success in dealing with conflict

We've seen how to deal destructively with conflict situations. Now let's take a look at constructive approaches.

1. **Approach the source.**   To effectively resolve conflicts, nothing will be as effective as a face-to-face meeting. E-mail will definitely not work; in fact it will probably make matters worse since it is so open to interpretation. To settle your differences, meet the other person face to face.

2. **Be constructive and retain control.** When you are in control of your emotions, rather than letting your emotions control you, you will be more able to influence a positive outcome. If someone is raising their voice and provoking an argument, and you stay cool and in control, then the disagreement will more than likely dissipate.

3. **Keep people and problems separate.** Very often the person behaving badly will use some of the behaviours listed above to distract your attention from the main issue. If you stay focused on the solution instead of on the other person, you will be better able to use appropriate tone and language, and you can also avoid damaging relationships.

4. **Be honest.** The best behaviour to use in any communication is to be honest and straightforward. Put your message across in the most direct and assertive way possible, while using a respectful tone and appropriate language. Treat the other person calmly and do your best to be courteous to one another, remaining constructive under pressure. Writing out a script and practising what you are going to say beforehand will always help.

5. **Listen first, talk second.** You have learned all about listening in Chapter 3. In a conflict situation, all your active listening skills will be put to the test. By listening carefully you are most likely to understand why the person is adopting his/her position.

6. **Explore options and seek solutions.** The whole emphasis in any conflict situation must be to figure out a solution. The end result must be to make things better, resolve a problem, improve a situation. Be open to the idea that other positions may exist, and that together you can discover the most helpful one.

7. **Assume the best.** We have mentioned many times the danger of making assumptions. However, in conflict situations, it's good to assume the other person means well, so that the emphasis will be placed on actions and solutions.

Aha! Moment

The more I speak, the worse a conflict situation can get. The more I listen, the more I achieve understanding and diffuse tension.

Try This

At the end of a working week, make a list of all the disagreements or conflicts you had, and with whom. Ask yourself what you did to tackle the problem, and how well it worked. Consider other options.

Conflict resolution in practice

Let's use these seven secrets of dealing constructively with conflict and put them into practice in a simple conflict situation. Here's what happens:

Nancy is very upset about a negative situation. She decides to talk to Mark about it. She's careful to watch her tone and language, and to be calm and in control.

Mark actively listens without emotion and tries to see the situation from Nancy's viewpoint.

Nancy feels good that she is being heard and understood. The negative energy is dissolved.

They both stay focused and keep cool. They use respectful language and tact. They explore the wider issues of what is involved.

They discuss rewarding solutions.

RESULT: Conflict is resolved. Relationships improve.

Myth Buster

If the person causing the friction is the boss, then there's nothing I can do. I have no choice but to put up with it.

Not so. Sometimes the boss is totally unaware of the friction he/she is causing, and if you use the right approach he/she could be very happy that you point out what's happening.

Here's a story from Shirley:

Looking back on when I was growing up with my parents, I remember that whenever a difficult situation or conflict occurred, my mother was not fond of talking about it. Instead she would put up her hand to stop any discussion, saying "Enough now!" So as a child I would just go to my room and dwell on the situation. She too was probably dwelling on what had happened. The problem was, nothing was ever resolved, because we never got to talk about it. So that's the habit I got into for most of my formative years. However, when I started work, experienced more, travelled overseas, and started teaching communication skills, I realised that talking is good.

After almost 10 years of living and working overseas, I went back home to work in the UK again, and I stayed with my mother. I noticed how different we were. She noticed a difference in me too. I remember a particular occasion when we'd had a disagreement, and she stormed off to the lounge to watch television. I went to my room and sat there thinking, "This is wrong. It can't lead to any good outcome. I know better now." So without waiting, I went into the lounge, sat quietly on the sofa and said, "Mum I'd like to talk to you about this." Mum, typically, reacted with the hand, staring straight ahead and saying, "I'm watching TV right now." I said, "No problem, I'll just sit here and read this magazine until you've finished." Mum breathed a heavy sigh and told me how long the programme would last, so I replied, "Mum, I'm going to sit here for as long as it takes until you and I discuss this. I don't want an argument, I just want to discuss it calmly." So I sat there. Pretty soon Mum got the message, and she turned off the TV.

I'll never forget our groundbreaking discussion that day. Oh, it wasn't easy, and yes there were tears. But neither of us raised our voices, we both put forward our points honestly but respectfully, and it led to a win-win resolution — and a great big hug! The best thing of all was that Mum and I had opened up to each other, we'd listened to each other, and we set the precedent for future misunderstandings and disagreements. Of course they still happened, but now we had a great formula to build on. A formula that worked. And our mother-daughter relationship grew all the more stronger for it.

 Aha! Moment

I listen. I talk. Things change.

Try This

Cast your mind back to an incident in your own life. When did you first know that you had a conflict? What clues were there that you did not recognise? Given the opportunity of hindsight, how could you have avoided or alleviated the conflict situation?

A five-step process for conflict resolution

Conflict in the workplace can be extremely destructive to effective teamwork. Managed in the wrong way, real and legitimate differences between people can quickly spiral out of control, resulting in situations where co-operation breaks down and the team's mission is threatened. This is particularly the case where the wrong approach to conflict resolution is used.

To calm these situations down, it helps to take a positive approach to conflict resolution, where discussion is courteous and non-confrontational, and the focus is on issues rather than on individuals. If this is done, then, as long as people listen carefully and explore facts, issues and possible solutions properly, conflict can often be resolved effectively.

Let's look in a little more detail at a successful conflict resolution process. It involves five main steps:

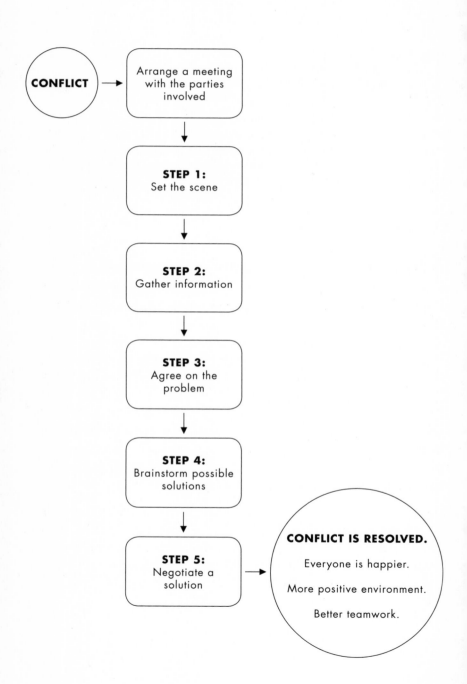

Step 1: Set the scene

Make sure you both understand that the conflict may be a mutual problem, and that it is best to resolve it through discussion and negotiation rather than through aggression. Emphasise the fact that you are presenting your perception of the problem. Use active listening skills — restate, paraphrase, summarise — to ensure you hear and understand the other person's viewpoints and perceptions. When you speak, use a mature, assertive approach rather than a submissive or aggressive style.

Step 2: Gather information

Try to identify the underlying interests, needs, and concerns. Let the other person know that you respect their opinion and need their co-operation to solve the problem. Ask for their viewpoints, and listen carefully. Listen with empathy and see the conflict from the other person's point of view. Identify issues clearly and concisely.

Try to understand the other person's motivations and goals, and see how your actions may be affecting these. Also, try to understand the conflict in objective terms: Is it affecting work performance? Is it damaging relationships with a client? Is it disrupting teamwork? Is it hindering decision-making? Remember to focus on work issues, and leave personalities out of the discussion. Problems, not people!

Step 3: Agree on the problem

Very often different underlying needs, interests and goals can cause people to perceive problems very differently. Before you can move on to find a mutually acceptable solution, it's important to agree on the problems that you are trying to solve. If you can't reach a common perception of the problem, then at the very least, you need to understand what the other person sees as the problem.

Step 4: Brainstorm possible solutions

It's always better if everyone concerned feels satisfied with the outcome, so make sure you both have a fair input in offering solutions. Brainstorm possible solutions, and be open to all ideas, including ones you never considered before.

Step 5: Negotiate and agree on a solution

By this stage, the conflict will hopefully be resolved: each may better understand the position of the other, and a mutually satisfactory solution may be clear to all. However, if you have uncovered real differences and deeper signs of conflict, then you may have to move forward into mediation where a third party is brought in to help resolve the situation.

Some sort of mediation is often necessary when a whole team is in conflict. Let's take a look at how the resolution process can be used for a team issue.

Dealing with team conflict

Whenever individuals come together as a team, it wouldn't be normal if there weren't any communication issues. They may be the result of personal friction between members, or because of the group dynamics as a whole. Whatever the cause, any unhealthy conflict will reduce the effectiveness of the team. Good communication skills can help to iron out conflicts and bring everyone together. Sometimes, however, a manager or mediator may have to step in.

Fast Fact

The first step in resolving team conflict is talking.

If you are the one who has to resolve the team conflict, the best thing to do at the outset is to speak to each team member individually. This will enable you to get to the root of the problem. You will need to ask specific questions of each person concerned, questions like:

"What is going wrong?"

"What do I need to know to understand the situation?"

"What do you think is the solution?"

"What do you think management should do about it?"

In these meetings, all your active listening and speaking skills will come to the fore. You will need to use empathy and assertiveness, as well as a good dose of patience and tact. Thank each person individually and tell them there will be a full group follow-up meeting with all concerned. This will help to make everyone feel valued, and they will have chance to prepare themselves.

Once you have met everyone concerned individually, bring the team together. Begin by emphasising the goals of the team, and point out the importance of solving the current problem. You may then proceed with these steps:

1. Agree on guidelines for behaviour during the meeting, including avoiding interrupting and managing and expressing emotions appropriately.

2. Summarise what you learned from your individual meetings.

3. Ask if the people involved agree with your summary of the situation, and seek clarification if they don't.

4. Don't allow their responses to turn into an argument, or a judgement of who is right or wrong. The main aim is to make sure each person understands the other person's viewpoint.

5. Ask each of them to discuss how the problem could be resolved.

6. Now you have the information you need to facilitate a group discussion of the changes that need to be made.

7. Ensure a commitment is received from each person about the changes agreed.

8. End positively by thanking them for their co-operation. Express your faith in everyone's ability to proceed positively and constructively.

It's possible that your conflict will take more than one meeting to resolve. If the meeting turns out to be too emotional, make the decision to adjourn until another time, so that people can calm down, and you or a mediator can choose a course of action. This may involve more one-on-one talks, or a workshop, or some high-level decision-making. Whatever the case, these decisions are best made when hearts and minds are relatively calm.

 Aha! Moment

> Conflict is inevitable whenever people work in teams. Dealing with it immediately and positively is essential.

Myth Buster

Team talks are only necessary whenever there is a communication breakdown.

On the contrary, just as the coach of a football team holds regular team talks, this is important in business organisations too. Team talks bring people together because they can be motivating, and they help people understand what's expected of them. They provide an opportunity for feedback so grievances aren't allowed to fester.

Conflict resolution brings many benefits

In most cases, effective conflict resolution skills can mean the difference between positive and extremely negative outcomes. By resolving conflict successfully, you will not only solve the problems that it brought to the surface, but you will also gain many other benefits:

- **Increased understanding.** The discussion needed to resolve conflict expands people's awareness of the situation, giving them an insight into how they can achieve their own goals without undermining those of other people.

- **Increased team cohesion.** When conflict is resolved effectively, team members can develop stronger mutual respect, and a renewed faith in their ability to work together.

- **Improved self-knowledge.** Conflict pushes individuals to examine their goals in closer detail, helping them understand the things that are most important to them, sharpening their focus, and enhancing their effectiveness.

- **Personal and professional growth.** Resolving conflict successfully increases your credibility, and you are likely to be given more responsibility in the organisation as a result.

Star Tips for dealing effectively with conflict

1. Deal with conflict as soon as you feel it. Don't let it fester. Sit down and talk when the first signs appear.

2. Keep a lookout for warning signs of friction, and learn to recognise them.

3. Don't use e-mail to resolve friction — it will rarely work.

4. Keep people and problems separate. Focus on issues rather than individuals.

5. Adopt a positive approach to conflict resolution.

6. Be courteous and respectful while using appropriate language in conflict resolution discussions.

7. Avoid shouting, swearing, sarcasm, insults, and other negative behaviour. This will just make matters worse.

8. Script and practise difficult discussions beforehand.

9. Use your active listening skills to achieve understanding and diffuse friction.

10. Remember to assume the best in conflict situations, so that the emphasis remains on actions and solutions.

INDEX

ABOUT THE AUTHORS

Shirley Taylor

Shirley Taylor has established herself as a leading authority in modern business writing and communication skills. She is the author of six successful books on communication skills, including the international bestseller, *Model Business Letters, E-mails and Other Business Documents*, which is now in its sixth edition, having sold almost half a million copies worldwide.

Shirley was born in the UK, and has lived and worked in Singapore, Bahrain and Canada. She has over 20 years of experience in teaching and training. After making Singapore her home in 2002, Shirley established her own company in 2007. ST Training Solutions Pte Ltd has quickly become highly regarded for providing a wide range of quality training programmes conducted by first-class trainers. The popularity of STTS workshops, and the keen desire of participants to learn more, is what originally led to this Success Skills series of books, which will prove an exciting supplement for those who are keen to develop their knowledge and skills.

Shirley conducts her own popular workshops on business writing and e-mail, as well as communication and secretarial skills. She puts a lot of passion and energy into her workshops to make sure they are entertaining, practical, informative, and a lot of fun.

Having learnt a lot from her workshop participants over the years, Shirley has put much of her experience into the pages of this book.

Shirley's book, *E-mail Etiquette: A fresh look at dealing effectively with e-mail, developing great style, and writing clear, concise messages*, is also part of the Success Skills series.

Alison Lester

Alison Lester, Director of AJ Lester Communication Training and an associate trainer with ST Training Solutions, has been specialising in developing communication, presentation and creativity training for clients in Asia and Europe since 1999.

Born in the United States, Alison draws much of her approach to communication skills training from her experience living, studying, and working in countries as diverse as the UK, China, Italy, Japan, France, and Singapore, stressing openness, clarity and flexibility. Given Shirley's international experience and similar philosophy, it was only natural, and a great pleasure, for them to come together to write this book.

Alison also employs her training as an improvisational comedian in her workshops and coaching sessions. This keeps things interesting and entertaining, and also helps participants gain greater confidence in their own ideas and greater facility in accessing them on the spot.

Alison's book, *Present for Success: A fresh, powerful approach to building confidence, developing impact and transforming all your presentations*, is also part of the Success Skills series. She also writes fiction, and her collection of short stories, *Locked Out: Stories Far from Home*, was published in Singapore in 2006.

ST Training Solutions

Success Skills Series

ST Training Solutions, based in Singapore, offers a wide range of popular, practical training programmes conducted by experienced, professional trainers. As CEO, Shirley Taylor takes a personal interest in working closely with trainers to ensure that each workshop is full of valuable tools, helpful guidelines and powerful action steps that will ensure a true learning experience for all participants. Some of the workshops offered are:

Power up your Business Writing Skills
Energise your E-mail Writing Skills
Success Skills for Secretaries and Support Staff
Successful Business Communication Skills
Creativity at Work
Present for Success
Speak up Successfully
Powerful People Skills
Get to Grips with Grammar
Activate your Listening Skills
Emotional Intelligence at Work
Business Etiquette and Professional Poise
Dealing with Difficult People and Situations
Achieving Peak Performance by Improving your Memory
Enhance your Productivity with Speed-reading
Personal Effectiveness and You
Projecting a Professional Image

Shirley Taylor is also host of a very popular annual conference called ASSAP — the Asian Summit for Secretaries and Admin Professionals — organised in April each year by ST Training Solutions.

Find out more about ST Training Solutions at www.shirleytaylortraining.com. Visit www.STSuccessSkills.com for additional resources.